NUUCHAHNULTH (NOOTKA)
MORPHOSYNTAX

Nuuchahnulth (Nootka) Morphosyntax

Toshihide Nakayama

UNIVERSITY OF CALIFORNIA PRESS
Berkeley • Los Angeles • London

UNIVERSITY OF CALIFORNIA PUBLICATIONS IN LINGUISTICS

Volume 134

UNIVERSITY OF CALIFORNIA PRESS
BERKELEY AND LOS ANGELES, CALIFORNIA

UNIVERSITY OF CALIFORNIA PRESS, LTD.
LONDON, ENGLAND

Library of Congress Cataloging-in-Publication Data

Nakayama, Toshihide, 1963–
Nuuchahnulth (Nootka) morphosyntax / Toshihide Nakayama.
p. cm. — (University of California publications in linguistics ; v. 134)
English and Nootka.
Includes bibliographical references.
ISBN 0-520-09841-2 (pbk.)
1. Nooka language—Morphosyntax. I. Title. II. Series.

PM2031 .N34 2001
497'.9—dc21 2001048054

For Kumiko, Erika,
and Maika

Contents

List of Tables, xiii

Acknowledgments, xv

Abbreviations and Conventions, xvii

1. Introduction 1
    1.1. About the Language, 1
    1.2. Previous Studies, 3
    1.3. About the Database, 3
    1.4. About the Writing System, 4
    1.5. Organization of This Grammar, 5

2. Overview of Phonology and Morphology 6
    2.1. Phoneme Inventory, 6
        2.1.1. Consonants, 6
        2.1.2. Vowels, 7
    2.2. Phonological Processes, 9
        2.2.1. Vowel Contraction, 9
        2.2.2. Labialization, 11
        2.2.3. Delabialization, 11
    2.3. Morphophonemics, 12
        2.3.1. Hardening, 12
        2.3.2. Softening, 14
        2.3.3. Lengthening, 15
        2.3.4. Reduplication, 15
    2.4. Morphology, 16
        2.4.1. Core vs. Peripheral Suffixes, 16
        2.4.2. Core Suffixes, 18
            2.4.2.1. Lexical Suffixes, 18

2.4.2.2. Aspect, 25
2.4.2.2.1. Momentaneous, 25
2.4.2.2.2. Durative, 26
2.4.2.2.3. Continuative, 26
2.4.2.2.4. Inceptive, 27
2.4.2.2.5. Iterative, 27
2.4.2.2.6. Graduative, 28
2.4.2.2.7. Repetitive, 28
2.4.3. Peripheral Suffixes, 29
2.4.3.1. Person, 29
2.4.3.2. Mood, 30
2.4.3.2.1. Indicative, 30
2.4.3.2.2. Interrogative, 31
2.4.3.2.3. Quotative, 31
2.4.3.2.4. Conditional, 32
2.4.3.2.5. Dubitative, 33
2.4.3.2.6. Purposive, 34
2.4.3.2.7. Subordinate, 35
2.4.3.2.8. Relative, 36
2.4.3.2.9. Indefinite Relative, 36
2.4.3.2.10. Imperative, 38
2.4.3.2.11. Placement of Mood Suffixes, 38
2.4.3.2.12. The Nature of Mood Suffixes, 43

3. The Nature of Word Classes and Word Formation 44
3.1. Word Classes, 44
3.1.1. Previous Studies, 44
3.1.1.1. Semantic Approaches, 45
3.1.1.2. A Structural Approach, 46
3.1.2. Word Classes in Nuuchahnulth, 47
3.1.2.1. Nominals and Verbals, 47
3.1.2.2. Adjectivals, 50
3.1.2.3. Other Previously Proposed Word Classes, 51
3.1.2.3.1. Adverbs?, 51
3.1.2.3.2. Prepositions?, 53
3.1.2.3.3. Auxiliary Verbs?, 54
3.1.2.4. Summary of the Proposed Word Classes, 56
3.1.2.5. The Nature of Word Classes in Nuuchahnulth, 57

3.2. Internal Structure of the Word, 58
3.2.1. Characteristics of Roots and Lexical Suffixes, 58
3.2.1.1. Roots, 58
3.2.1.2. Lexical Suffixes, 59
3.2.2. Types of Relationships between Stems and Lexical Suffixes, 64
3.2.2.1. Object + Predicate, 64
3.2.2.2. Complement + Higher Predicate, 64
3.2.2.3. Modifier + Nominal, 65
3.2.2.4. Numeral + Classifier, 66
3.2.2.5. Predicate + Adverbial, 67
3.2.3. On the Nature of Morphological Complexity, 68

4. The Structural Organization of Nuuchahnulth Syntax 69
4.1. Relationships between Words, 69
4.1.1. Argumenthood, 70
4.1.2. Modification, 71
4.1.3. Serialization, 71
4.1.4. Complementation, 72
4.2. Domains of Syntactic Patterning, 72
4.2.1. The Clause, 73
4.2.2. The Phrase, 76
4.2.2.1. Nominal phrase, 76
4.2.2.2. Verbal Phrase, 79
4.2.2.3. The Nature of the Domain, 80
4.2.3. Predication, 80
4.3. Argument Structure, 83
4.3.1. Argument Structure in Nuuchahnulth, 85
4.3.2. Characteristics of Arguments in Nuuchahnulth, 86
4.3.2.1. Subjects, 86
4.3.2.2. Objects, 87
4.4. General Structure-Building Strategies, 89
4.4.1. Expansion of Nominals, 90
4.4.1.1. Nominal Concatenation, 90
4.4.1.2. Modification, 90
4.4.1.2.1. Types of Modification, 91
4.4.1.2.2. General Organizational Principles, 91
4.4.1.2.3. Meanings Added through Modificational Expansion, 93
4.4.1.2.3.1. Quantifiers, 93

4.4.1.2.3.2. Numerals, 93
4.4.1.2.3.3. Property Concepts, 94
4.4.1.2.3.4. Event / State, 94
4.4.1.2.3.5. Location, 96
4.4.2. Expansion of Verbals, 97
4.4.2.1. Serialization, 97
4.4.2.1.1. Function of Serialization, 99
4.4.2.1.2. Meanings Expressed with Serialization, 102
4.4.2.1.2.1. Action + Location, 102
4.4.2.1.2.2. Action + Time, 103
4.4.2.1.2.3. Action + Manner, 104
4.4.2.1.2.4. Action + Action, 105
4.4.2.1.2.5. Action + Relational, 106
4.4.2.1.3. Structural Relationship between Serialized Clauses, 109
4.4.2.1.4. Relative Ordering of Serialized Clauses, 113
4.4.2.2. Modification, 113
4.4.2.3. Complementation, 114
4.4.2.3.1. Complement-Taking Predicates, 114
4.4.2.3.1.1. Clauses as Complements, 115
4.4.2.3.1.2. Predications as complements, 117
4.4.2.3.2. Negation, 119
4.4.2.3.3. Nonpolar Questions, 122
4.5. The Manipulation of Participant Structure, 123
4.5.1. Causatives, 123
4.5.2. Possession, 128
4.5.3. Perspective-Shifting, 133
4.5.3.1. Types of Effects on the Participant Configuration, 134
4.5.3.1.1. Perspective Reversal, 134
4.5.3.1.2. Undergoer-Centralized Perspective-Setting, 138
4.5.3.1.3. Departicularization, 139
4.5.3.1.3.1. Generic Statements, 139
4.5.3.1.3.2. Instructive Expressions, 140
4.5.3.1.3.3. Nonspecific Actions, 141
4.5.3.2. The Nature of the Effects of the Perspective-Shifting, 142
4.6. Patterns of Encoding of the Participant Configuration in Discourse, 143
4.6.1. Morphological vs. Syntactic Encoding of Participants, 143
4.6.2. Simplex vs. Complex Predication, 145

4.7. The Ordering of Arguments, 148
4.7.1. Relative Ordering within a Clause, 149
4.7.1.1. Ordering between Argument and Predicate, 149
4.7.1.2. Ordering between Arguments, 150
4.7.2. The Domain of Argument Placement, 151

Afterword, 155

References, 159

Tables

1. List of Textual Materials, 4
2. Consonant Inventory, 7
3. Nootkan Cognates, 7
4. Pattern for Use of -*'at*, 137

Acknowledgments

This book was made possible by countless people throughout my graduate career. Instead of making an impossible attempt to list the names of all the people who deserve thanks, I mention only those who helped me most directly with the completion of this project.

I would like to thank my primary Nuuchahnulth teachers, the late George Louie and Caroline Little, for patiently working to help me understand the language and for sharing their knowledge about the old ways of the Nuuchahnulth people. Both of the elders have devoted much time and energy to preserving the linguistic and cultural knowledge of Nuuchahnulth. In addition, the following elders generously took their time to participate in the project: the late James Adams, the late Harold Little, Archie Thompson, and Josephine Thompson. I would also like to thank Katie Frazer and Luuta Qamiina for their patient assistance in transcribing and translating the collected texts. All of these people are working hard in their own ways as part of the larger effort to preserve and pass on the language and culture of the Nuuchahnulth to future generations, and I hope that this book can make a meaningful contribution to this effort.

On the academic side, my sincere thanks go to Wally Chafe, William Jacobsen, Marianne Mithun, and Sandy Thompson. I would like to express my special gratitude to Thom Hess of the University of Victoria, who gave me the opportunity to work with Nuuchahnulth and has been helpful and encouraging in countless ways since then, and to Osahito Miyaoka of Kyoto University, who first introduced me to Native American linguistics and who has provided constant support and encouragement across the Pacific Ocean. I would also like to thank the Editorial Board of the UCPL series and the anonymous reviewers for their invaluable comments.

Support for trips to the field and for work on the book was provided in part by the following agencies: American Philosophical Society, Phillips Fund (1992–93, 1998); Jacobs Research Funds (1992–95); University of California, Santa Barbara: Graduate Division, Department of Linguistics, General Affiliates; Summer Institute of Linguistics (SIL Fund for Scholarly Advancement, Program for Research on Endangered Languages [1995]); the Japanese Ministry of Education, Science and Culture, International Scientific Research Program (1992–99) through grants for the projects 'Linguistic Fieldwork of Northwestern North American Natives' and 'Urgent Linguistic Fieldwork of the North Pacific Rim' (Osahito Miyaoka, principal investigator). I would also like to thank the

Department of Linguistics at the University of Victoria and the Royal British Columbia Museum for their cooperation during my field research.

Finally, I would like to thank my family for what I have been able to accomplish. I truly don't know how to thank my wife Kumiko, who not only made, with a smile of understanding, a tremendous sacrifice in order to accommodate my research activities and to secure my writing time, but also gave me unwavering support and encouragement. And the smile of my little daughters Erika and Maika melted away the most stressful moments and gave me strength to continue writing.

Toshihide Nakayama

June 2001

Abbreviations and Conventions

The following abbreviations are used in glosses:

CAUS	causative
COND	conditional
CONT	continuative
DEF	definite
DIM	diminutive
DUB	dubitative
DUP	reduplicational prefix (CV of a root)
DUR	durative
REDUP	reduplicational prefix (whole root)
EVID	evidential
FUT	future
GRAD	graduative
IMP	imperative
INC	inceptive
IND	indicative
INDF	indefinite
INF	inferential
INTER	interrogative
ITER	iterative
LOC	locative root
MOM	momentaneous
MOMCAUS	momentaneous causative
POSS	possessive
PL	plural
PURP	purposive
QUOT	quotative
REL	relative
RELDUB	relative dubitative
REP	repetitive
SHIFT	perspective-shifting suffix
SIM	simultaneous
SUB	subordinate
TEL	telic

About Glossing

For most examples interlinear glosses are provided. The interlinear glosses consist of a line showing the morphological makeup of words and a line for morpheme-by-morpheme glosses. For many examples I also provide a line indicating the word-level translations. The word-level translations are provided for the readers' convenience. However, they are often arbitrary and artificial because of the fundamental differences between Nuuchahnulth and English. Therefore, it is better to rely on the word-level translations as little as possible when reading examples. Word-level translations are not provided for examples in which these translations would be grossly misleading.

1

INTRODUCTION

The main goal of this study is to provide a general account of morphosyntactic structuring in the Nuuchahnulth language that is not only accurate in terms of observable facts but also appropriate and sensible in terms of the overall typological characteristics of Nuuchahnulth and the discourse-functional motivations. Linguistic patterns are 'situated' in the structural and functional environment in that they are shaped and maintained in interaction between structural and functional forces. Aiming at capturing the overall structural dynamics in Nuuchahnulth, I pay special attention to 'appropriateness' and 'sensibility' of the description in the structural and functional environment.

Typologically Nuuchahnulth is dramatically different from widely studied European languages to such an extent that a simple comparison between these languages and Nuuchahnulth is in many cases misleading. This fact presents a serious challenge to the study of Nuuchahnulth in frameworks developed in the Western linguistic tradition. Many of the concepts and categories that form the foundation of modern linguistic descriptions and theories have been developed and established in the study of European languages; not surprisingly, they reflect the structural environment of those languages. If we were to apply the same concepts and categories uncritically to phenomena in Nuuchahnulth, our description would not capture the real structural dynamics of Nuuchahnulth. Thus, this study involves an extensive reexamination and reformulation of some fundamental concepts in linguistics.

This study is data-driven. The description that is presented here is based exclusively on natural discourse data: it can be verified by patterns found in actual language use.

1.1. About the Language

A word about the name of the language is in order. The people who have been designated by the name *Nootka* object to this designation. Traditionally Nuuchahnulth tribes did not have a native word that included the whole group. The word *Nootka* was first used for them by Captain Cook when he made contact with the people, apparently mistaking the word *nuutxaa* 'circling about' as the tribal name (Walbran 1909; Drucker 1951). After the Nuuchahnulth people formed their political organization in 1958, the West Coast Allied Tribes (later called the West Coast District Council), they referred to themselves for many years simply as *West Coast* (Arima and Dewhirst 1990). In 1978 they devised the name *Nuuchahnulth*[1] (*nuučaańuɬ* 'all along the mountains'), and since then it has been their preferred name for themselves and their language.

Note that *Nuuchahnulth* is not an exact equivalent of *Nootka* as a linguistic designation, since it includes the related but separate language Ditidaht. This makes the term *Nuuchahnulth* a less ideal alternative in the context of linguistic description. Nevertheless, I respect the decision of the Nuuchahnulth people and avoid the designation *Nootka* in this book. Note, however, that the description presented here concerns only the language formerly known as Nootka and not Ditidaht. Thus, in this book the designation *Nuuchahnulth* should be understood as a reference to the language formerly known as *Nootka*, not including Ditidaht.

The Nuuchahnulth language is spoken by several hundred people on the west coast of Vancouver Island, British Columbia, Canada. Nuuchahnulth, together with Ditidaht (formerly Nitinaht or Nitinat) and Makah, constitute the Southern Wakashan (or Nootkan) branch of the Wakashan language family. Within the southern branch, the relationship between Ditidaht and Makah is generally considered close, with the separation time depth of about 1,000 years (Jacobsen 1979b). The Northern Wakashan branch includes Haisla, Heiltsuk-Oowekyala, and Kwak'wala.

There are 15 officially recognized bands within Nuuchahnulth, but the exact number of dialects cannot be determined at this point. The data used in this book are from the Ahousaht dialect, which is spoken in the central part of the Nuuchahnulth-speaking area.

Unfortunately, the Nuuchahnulth language is at present in danger of being lost, as a result of rapid and far-reaching acculturation. There are very few, if any, monolingual speakers of Nuuchahnulth left. Most people below the age of 60 do not speak or understand the language at all, which is making revival of the language extremely difficult.

The syntactic structure of Nuuchahnulth has many unique characteristics that find no comparison in any of the well-studied European languages. The differences are often significant enough to force us to reconsider widely accepted syntactic notions. With its extremely weak lexical categories, relatively fluid word order, and active polysynthesis revolving around numerous suffixes with lexical meanings, syntactic structures in Nuuchahnulth do not seem to be as clearly defined as in European languages. In European languages syntactic structures appear to be much more clearly established on the basis of grammaticized lexical categories and morphological markers for various

[1] This spelling convention was officially adopted by the Nuuchahnulth Tribal Council and is widely used as the official spelling of the tribal name.

grammatical relations. To look at this from another angle, syntactic structures in European languages appear to have been grammaticized to a much greater extent in the form of well-defined lexical categories and morphological markers for grammatical relations. In Nuuchahnulth, on the other hand, there is little formal anchoring of syntactic structures in the form of grammaticized classes or markers. This is, of course, not to say that there is no structure at the syntactic level in Nuuchahnulth. In fact, natural discourse data show that there are reasonably clear structural regularities in the syntactic patterning in the language. However, the lack of formal anchoring most certainly presents a major challenge in identifying and describing the structural regularities found in Nuuchahnulth syntax.

1.2. Previous Studies

The first extensive linguistic data collection from Nuuchahnulth was done by the eminent linguist Edward Sapir around the turn of the twentieth century. The material was collected from southern dialects, mainly Tseshaht, and includes vocabulary and texts that range from traditional tales to ethnographic narratives. The collected texts have been published in Sapir (1924) and Sapir and Swadesh (1939, 1955). However, much of Sapir's material is still in the form of unpublished field notes (archived in the Franz Boas Collection at the American Philosophical Society). Swadesh (1933, 1939) provides a grammatical description of the southern dialects that mainly covers the word-building process. There are also journal articles that highlight specific aspects of the grammar (Sapir 1915; Swadesh 1948; Jacobsen 1969a, 1969b; Haas 1969a, 1969b; Klokeid and Mooney 1970; Haas 1972; Klokeid 1975; Rose 1976; Jacobsen 1979a; Whistler 1980, 1985; Emanatian 1988; Jacobsen 1993).

There is in addition a large collection of stories and texts from a northern dialect, Kyuquot, made in the late 1970s by Suzanne Rose. However, the material has never been published. Rose (1981) provides a comprehensive description of Kyuquot.

As for the central dialects, including Ahousaht, published information consists of articles on specific aspects of the grammar (Nakayama 1994, 1995a, 1995b, 1997b).

1.3. About the Database

This book is based on natural discourse data that I collected during five summers of field work. Although I sometimes use constructed examples in this work, use of such examples is limited to illustrating a pattern with structurally simple examples.

The database for this book consists of 12 texts told in the Ahousaht dialect, including 9 relatively long (15- to 40-minute) narratives (personal, historical, and traditional) and three conversation segments (about 5 minutes each). These texts were collected from three native speakers who were in their seventies and eighties. The texts have been transcribed and translated into English with the assistance of native speakers, resulting in approximately 4,400 lines of textual material. The list of textual materials used in this book is given in Table 1.

Table 1: List of Textual Materials

Title	**Genre**	**Length** (# of lines)
CANOE	Technical narrative	512
CLLS	Personal narrative	668
DOG	Traditional narrative	172
ECLIPSE	Ethnographic narrative	27
GLLS	Personal narrative	308
GRAY WHALE	Ethnographic narrative	24
JG.I	Conversation	28
JG.II	Conversation	95
KINGFISHER	Historical narrative	591
LESSON	Ethnographic narrative	190
LITTLES.I	Conversation	94
MINK	Traditional narrative	729
POTLATCH	Ethnographic narrative	49
QAWIQAALTH	Traditional narrative	394
WOLF	Ethnographic narrative	500

1.4. About the Writing System

The symbols used for representation of Nuuchahnulth forms in this book generally follow the writing system widely used by Nuuchahnulth tribes, which is in turn based on the variant of the Americanists' phonetic alphabet that is in use among the local linguists. The only deviation in my system from the popular writing system concerns the length distinction in underlying vowels. Thus, a LONG vowel is indicated as ***V:*** (colon) and a variable-length vowel as ***V·*** (raised dot). Note that this distinction is only relevant in the underlying representation and therefore is not indicated in the surface form. Long surface vowels are indicated as ***VV***, following the popular convention, regardless of the underlying length feature.

1.5. Organization of This Grammar

The main part of this book is organized as follows. In Chapter 2, I present a brief sketch of the basic phonological and morphological facts about Nuuchahnulth. Chapter 3 discusses the domain of a word, in order to establish a structural environment in which the description of syntactic regularities and structures should be situated. The characteristics of the domain of the word, e.g., what can be encoded at the word level and how words can be classified in terms of behavioral and functional characteristics, have significant implications for the way words are associated at the syntax level and also for the functional loads that the syntax-level structuring carries. In this sense the discussion concerning the nature of words in Chapter 3 is an important part of an attempt to attain an accurate and realistic description of syntactic structuring in Nuuchahnulth. Finally, in Chapter 4, I discuss the nature of syntactic structuring as well as different structural strategies of building complex syntactic constructions in Nuuchahnulth.

2

OVERVIEW OF PHONOLOGY AND MORPHOLOGY

In this chapter I present a brief overview of phonological and morphological facts about Nuuchahnulth, mainly as a preparation for the discussion of syntactic patterning in the main part of this book.

2.1. Phoneme Inventory

2.1.1. Consonants

Nuuchahnulth, as a language in the Northwest Coast cultural-linguistic area, is not an exception in having a large inventory of consonants, some of which are relatively uncommon outside the area. Phonological features shared with other languages in the area include: an ejective series; opposition of rounded/unrounded velars and uvulars; fricatives in many positions; lateral obstruents. (For more on the areal linguistic features of the Northwest Coast, see Thompson and Kinkade 1990; Sherzer 1976). The inventory of Nuuchahnulth consonants is given in Table 2.

Glottal resonants are pronounced as resonants with preglottalization. The pharyngeal consonants are pronounced with a constriction or closure made at or near the pharynx. They greatly affect the quality of the following vowel.

The sounds that are presented above in parentheses, *x̣* and $\dot{q}^w$, are extremely rare. Historically the ejectives and fricatives at the uvular region shifted into the pharyngeal stops and fricatives ($*\dot{q}$, $*\dot{q}^w$ > ʕ; **x̣*, $*\underset{\cdot}{x}^w$ > *ḥ*), and it is probable that *x̣* and $\dot{q}^w$ have been reintroduced through borrowings from neighboring languages (see Jacobsen 1969b). In the process of development of pharyngeals from uvulars the contrast of labialization was lost, leaving only the nonlabialized sounds in the pharyngeal region. A trace of this labialization contrast, however, can still be observed in the morphophonemics of the language: under the morphophonological condition of 'hardening' some instances of *ḥ* undergo the same change as other labialized consonants, while others do not. (For detailed discussion of 'hardening', see 2.3.1.) This fact may justify recognition of an abstract phoneme /ḥʷ/ separately from /ḥ/, although it is never realized as such on the surface (see Rose 1976). Within Nootkan this development of pharyngeals from uvulars occurred in Nuuchahnulth and partially in Ditidaht, where only the pharyngeal stop developed (see Table 3).

Table 2: Consonant Inventory

	LABIAL	APICAL	ALVEOLAR	LATERAL	PALATAL	VELAR	LABIO-VELAR	UVULAR	LABIO-UVULAR	PHARYNGEAL	GLOTTAL
STOPS	*p*	*t*	*c*	*ƛ*	*č*	*k*	*kʷ*	*q*	*qʷ*	ʕ	ʔ
EJECTIVES	*p̓*	*t̓*	*c̓*	*ƛ̓*	*č̓*	*k̓*	*k̓ʷ*		(*q̓ʷ*)		
FRICATIVES			*s*	*ɬ*	*š*	*x*	*xʷ*	(*x̣*)		*ḥ*	*h*
RESONANTS	*m*	*n*			*y*		*w*				
GLOTTAL RESONANTS	*m̓*	*n̓*			*y̓*		*w̓*				

Table 3: Nootkan Cognates (Source: Haas n.d.)

Nuuchahnulth		Ditidaht		Makah		
ʕ	*ʕaɬuu*	ʕ	*ʕaɬaw*	*q̓*	*q̓aɬaw*	'beaver'
ʕ	*ʕaanus*	ʕ	*ʕaalis*	*q̓ʷ*	*q̓ʷaalis*	'crane'
ḥ	*ʔatḥii*	*x̣*	*ʔatx̣ii*	*x̣*	*ʔatx̣ii*	'night'
ḥ	*ɬuḥc̓iɬi*	*x̣ʷ*	*ɬux̣ʷ-*	*x̣ʷ*	*ɬux̣ʷuučid*	'head'

2.1.2. Vowels

In sharp contrast with the complex consonant system, the vowel system in Nuuchahnulth is relatively simple. Ahousaht Nuuchahnulth has three phonemic vowel qualities, /i, a, u/

and a two-way length distinction. Vowel qualities [ɛ] and [ɔ] also occur, but only marginally in certain formulaic expressions or as stylistic variants of *i* and *u*, respectively.

(1) [ɛ] and [ɔ] in formulaic expressions:

ƛakoo [ƛakɔː] 'thank you'

xemc [xɛmts] closing expression used in storytelling
(in a repeated form *xemc xemc xemc*)

(2) [ɛ] and [ɔ] as stylistic variants:

a. [hi:tinqsaʔɛː]
hitinqsaˀi
hita -inq -'sa(ƛ) -'i·
get.there -being.down.a.slope-getting.on.the.beach -IMP.2s

'Come down to the beach.' (e.g., when calling out) [Mink 272]

b. [ɬuɬu:čmɔːp]
ɬuɬuučmuup
DUP *-ɬu:čmu:p*
DISTR -sister

'sisters' (e.g., when calling out) [Potlach 1]

On the surface Ahousaht vowels can be realized as either long or short, but underlyingly the distinction is three-way, i.e., LONG, VARIABLE-LENGTH, and SHORT. The difference between LONG and VARIABLE-LENGTH is not length but a distribution pattern on the surface. A LONG vowel (indicated in underlying forms as ***V:***) is always realized as long, whereas a VARIABLE-LENGTH vowel (indicated as ***V·***) is long if it occurs in the first or second syllable, but short otherwise.

(3) LONG vowel

a. in the first or second syllable:
*ˀat**quu***
*ˀat -**qu:***
although -COND.3

'although' [CLLS 11]

b. in the third syllable or later:
*muuˀaƛ**quu***
*mu: -'aƛ -**qu:***
four -TEL -COND.3

'There used to be four.' [CLLS 34]

(4) VARIABLE-LENGTH vowel

a. in the first or second syllable:
ʔiiḥtuup
ʔi:ḥʷ-tu·p
big -species

'whale' [elicited 8.4.92-35]

b. in the third syllable or later:
quʔactup
quʔac-tu·p
person-species

'human being' [Mink 21]

It has been suggested that the VARIABLE-LENGTH phenomenon represents an unmarked case and that the persistently long vowels developed later (Jacobsen 1979b; Klokeid 1975). According to this view, there has been a general process of vowel shortening that affects vowels in the third or later syllable, but this process does not apply to long vowels that have developed later. Thus, this distinction between LONG and VARIABLE-LENGTH represents different historical layers in the vowel system.

2.2. Phonological Processes

2.2.1. Vowel Contraction

Vowels that occur adjacent to each other are regularly contracted into a single vowel segment. The quality of the resulting vowel is determined by the vowel higher in the hierarchy *u* > *i* > *a*: thus, the resulting vowel is *u* if either of the vowels is *u*, *i* if both are not u and either vowel is *i*, and *a* otherwise.

(5) ***u*** has priority over ***i***

a. ***u+i* → *u***
ňupuuɬ
ňupu -i·ɬ
six -fathoms

'six fathoms'
[Canoe 22]

b. ***i+u* → *u***
ʔukčumyiɬʔaƛquus
ʔu -(k)či -umɬ -'iɬ -'aƛ -qu:s
it -being.with -being.in.a.group -being.in.the.house-TEL -COND.1sg

'I would be on the floor with her.'
[CLLS 175]

(6) ***u*** has priority over ***a***

a. ***u+a → u***

*ˀ**u**yiiˀat*
*ˀ**u** -**a**yi· -'at*
it -giving -SHIFT
'They give it to him.'
[Dog 9]

b. ***a+u → u***

*ċaaw**u**mɬ*
*ċaw**a** -**u**mɬ*
one -being.in.a.group
'There is only one in a group.'
[Mink 264]

(7) ***i*** has priority over ***a***

a. ***a+i → i***

*sučii**ɬ***
*suč**a** -**i**·ɬ*
five -fathoms
'five fathoms'
[Canoe 22]

b. ***i+a → i***

hiẏakƛiqsˀi
*hiɬ -'akƛ**i** -**a**qs -ˀi·*
be.there -being.at.the.rear -being.in.a.canoe -DEF
'the stern'
[Canoe 221]

In terms of length, the vowel resulting from contraction has the feature of the longer vowel: i.e., [LONG] and [VARIABLE-LENGTH] always prevail over [SHORT]. The hierarchy between [LONG] and [VARIABLE-LENGTH] cannot be determined at this point because of lack of relevant data.

(8) [SHORT] + [VARIABLE-LENGTH]

*huˀ**aa**qtu*
*huˀ**a**-**a**·qtu·*
back -going.over.the.hill
'go back over the hill' [Kingfisher 165]

(9) [VARIABLE-LENGTH] + [SHORT]

*ċaw**ii**sta*
*ċaw**a**· -**i**sta*
one -persons.in.canoe
'go out alone in a canoe' [CLLS 74]

(10) [LONG] + [SHORT]

*naˀ**aa**taḥ*
*naˀ**a:**-**a**taḥ*
hear -trying.to.catch
'listen carefully' [Qawiqaalth 29]

(11) [SHORT] + [LONG]

*ˀaˀay**ii**p*
DUP- *ˀay**a** -**i:**p*
DISTR-many-obtaining
'He got many.' [GLLS 100]

When two short vowels are contracted to a single vowel in the first syllable of the root, the resulting vowel is [VARIABLE-LENGTH], rather than the expected [SHORT].

(12) ***ˀuuqstii***
ˀu -aqsti·
it -being.among
'among them' [Wolf 20]

2.2.2. Labialization

Nonlabialized consonants that have labialized counterparts, i.e., /k/, /k̓/, /q/, and /x/, become labialized following /u/ or /u:/.

(13) ***k → kʷ***
*haˀu**k̓ʷ**ap̓aƛ*
haˀuk -'ap -'aƛ
eat -CAUS -TEL
'feed them' [Canoe 112]

(14) ***q → qʷ***
*maakˀatu**qʷ**atup.*
makʷ -ˀatuq -'atup
trade -leaving.off -doing.for
'for sale' [CLLS 97]

2.2.3. Delabialization

Labialized consonants lose labialization before a consonant, the vowel /u/, and a word boundary.

(15)

a. before a consonant
*c̓u**qʷ**-* 'stab'
→ *c̓u**q**swii* [< *c̓u**qʷ**-* 'stab' + *-swi·* 'extending through'] 'stab through'
compare with: *c̓u**qʷ**aas* [< *c̓u**qʷ**-* 'stab' + *-a·s* 'being on a platform'] 'stab on a board'

b. before a consonant
*ˁa**xʷ**-* 'ebb, (tide) recede'
→ *ˁa**x**šiƛ* [< *ˁa**xʷ**-* 'ebb' + *-šiƛ* MOM] 'ebb, (tide) recede'
compare with: *ˁaxʷaa* [< *ˁaxʷ-* 'ebb' + *-(y)a·* DUR] '(tide) receding'

c. before /*u*/
mak^w- 'trade'
→ *makuuw̓as* [< *mak*^{w}- 'trade' + -*u·ɬ* 'place for' + -'*as* 'being outside'] 'store'
compare with: *maak*^{w}*aaʔatu* [< *mak*^{w}- 'trade' + -*a·ʔatu* 'coming off'] 'buy'

d. before a word boundary
ʔink^w- 'fire'
→ *ʔink* 'fire'
compare with: *ʔink*^{w}*iɬ* [< *ʔink*^{w}- 'fire' + -'*iɬ* 'being in the house'] 'in the house'

An interesting case is when a sound with a labialized counterpart is surrounded by /u/ as in the second *k* in *nuuknuukuk* 'songs', where the labialization and delabialization rules could interact depending on the relative ordering between them. If the labialization and delabialization rules apply in that order, the sound would first be labialized (since it occurs after /u:/) and then undergo delabialization (since it would be a labialized consonant occurring before /u/), resulting in a nonlabialized sound. The rules applied in the opposite order, however, would result in a labialized sound. In this type of situation, the sound in question indeed seems to be pronounced without labialization, which suggests that the labialization rule applies first.

2.3. Morphophonemics

Certain suffixes induce changes in the adjacent segment of the stem (HARDENING and SOFTENING) or in the overall shape of the stem (LENGTHENING, SHORTENING, and REDUPLICATION). The change induced is lexically specified for each suffix and cannot be predicted by a general principle.

2.3.1. Hardening

Some suffixes induce 'HARDENING' (Sapir and Swadesh 1939) of the immediately preceding stem consonant. The HARDENING changes stops, affricates, and resonants into their glottalized counterparts, and fricatives into /y̓/ or /w̓/ depending on the roundedness feature of the sound. In this book HARDENING suffixes are indicated by the diacritic ' (apostrophe) at the beginning, as in -'*as* 'being on the ground'.

(16) on a stop: ***k*** → ***k̓***
wik̓aḥs
wik-'aḥs
not -being.in.a.vessel
'nothing in a canoe' [Canoe 66]

(17) on an affricate: ***c*** → ***c̓***
quˀac̓aqƛ̓
quˀac -'aqƛ̓
human -being.inside
'There is a man inside.' [Canoe 9]

(18) on a resonant: ***m*** → ***m̓***
ˀaˀam̓iḥtaˀi.
DUP- *ˀam -'iḥta* -*ˀi·*
DISTR-LOC -being.at.the.end-DEF
'the ends' [Canoe 187]

(19) on a fricative
a. ***ɬ*** → ***y̓*** [unrounded consonant]
hiy̓aqƛ̓
hiɬ -'aqƛ̓
be.there -being.inside
'inside' [Canoe 10]

b. ***xʷ*** → ***w̓*** [rounded consonant]
ˀuw̓iiƛ̓
ˀuxʷ -'i·ƛ̓
topple.over -getting.on.the.ground
'it fell on the ground' [Canoe 8]

Uvular sounds, which do not have glottal counterparts, change into pharyngeals through HARDENING. This fact suggests that pharyngeals are functioning as glottalized uvulars in the phonological system of Nuuchahnulth.

(20) *ḥuˁitap*
ḥuq -'itap
hallowed.object -placing.on.the.ground
'He put a hallowed object (canoe) down on the ground.' [Canoe 116]

(21) *w̓ašˁaqƛ̓asna,*
w̓ašq -'aqƛ̓as -na·
bunched.together -being.in.the.house-1pl
'It was crowded in our house.' [CLLS 7]

The pharyngeal fricative /ḥ/ generally resists the effect of HARDENING as in (22) and (23). However, /ḥ/ in some morphemes is affected by HARDENING and changes into /w̓/ as illustrated in (24) and (25). This fact may justify recognition of a separate abstract phoneme /ḥʷ/ although it is never realized as such on the surface (see Rose 1976).

(22) *čiḥˀaqƛ̓*
čiḥ -ʼaqƛ̓
spirit -being.inside
'There is a spirit inside.' [Canoe 15]

(23) *ƛ̓aḥˀiiƛ̓*
ƛ̓aḥ -ʼi·(ƛ̓)
curled.up -getting.on.the.ground
'It bent down to the ground.' [Wolf 119]

(24) *ˀiiw̓aqstuƛ̓aˁaƛ̓*
ˀi:ḥʷ-ʼaqstu(ƛ̓) -aq -ʼaƛ̓
large -getting.inside -very -TEL
'It has became very expensive.' [CLLS 242]

(25) *kuw̓iiƛ̓*
kuḥʷ -ʼi·(ƛ̓)
opening -getting.on.the.ground
'It opened.' [GLLS 32]

When the stem ends with a vowel, the HARDENING suffix inserts /ʔ/ after the vowel.

(26) *ˀuˀiic*
ˀu -ʼi·c
it -consuming
'having it for a meal' [CLLS 165]

(27) *kʷaˀiiƛ̓*
kʷa -ʼi·(ƛ̓)
sit.down -getting.on.the.ground
'He is sitting down on the ground.' [Mink 198]

2.3.2. Softening

Some suffixes induce 'SOFTENING' (Sapir and Swadesh 1939), where the preceding fricative is changed into /y/ or /w/ depending on the roundedness feature of the sound. The SOFTENING suffix is indicated by the diacritic ' (open single quote).

(28) *š* → *y* [unrounded consonant]
p̓iyačiƛ̓
p̓iš -'ači(ƛ̓)
bad -INC
'It becomes bad.' [Kingfisher 49]

(29) ***ɬ*** → ***y*** [unrounded consonant]
hiišumyipiiɬ
hiš -umɬ -'iɬ
all -being.in.a.group -being.in.a.house
'get together in a house' [CLLS 270]

(30) ***ḥʷ*** → ***w*** [rounded consonant]
ʔiiwačiƛ̓.
ʔi:ḥʷ-'ačiƛ̓
large -INC
'It became large.' [Mink 188]

2.3.3. Lengthening

Some suffixes lengthen the first vowel of the stem. In (31) a LENGTHENING suffix *-i:ɬ* 'making' causes lengthening of the first vowel of the stem *č̓apac* 'canoe'. Similarly, the suffix *-'aɬuk* 'looking after' in (32) lengthens the first vowel of *wik* 'not'.

(31) *č̓**aa**paciiɬ*
*č̓apac **-i:ɬ***
canoe -making
'make a canoe' [Canoe 222]

(32) *w**ii**k̓aɬuk*
*wik-**'aɬuk***
not -looking.after
'not putting one's mind on [something]' [Canoe 223]

2.3.4. Reduplication

Some suffixes induce REDUPLICATION of the stem syllable.

(33) ***ciciqinkat***
ciq -ink -'at
speak -conversing.with -SHIFT
'have a conversation' [Canoe 6]

(34) ***tu****tušk̓iiḥ*
tušk -'i:ḥ
cod -hunting.for
'fishing cod' [Qawiqaalth 146]

2.4. Morphology

2.4.1. Core vs. Peripheral Suffixes

Suffixes in Nuuchahnulth can be divided into two general classes, which will be called CORE and PERIPHERAL suffixes in this work.[1] The two groups of suffixes are distinguished on the basis of several morphophonological and semantic criteria that are laid out below.

Phonologically, the effect on the stem triggered by core suffixes is stronger than that triggered by peripheral suffixes. First, the hardening effect triggered by core suffixes affects a wider range of consonants than that triggered by peripheral suffixes: specifically, core hardening suffixes affect fricatives as well as stops, affricates, and resonants, whereas peripheral hardening suffixes do not. Compare the following examples:

(35) CORE suffix: fricative is affected
hiy̓aḥs
hiɬ ***-'aḥs***
be.there -being.in.a.vessel
'inside a canoe' [Canoe 53]

(36) PERIPHERAL suffix: fricative resists the effect
hiɬʔaƛ
hiɬ ***-'aƛ***
be.there -TEL
'He was there.' [Dog 59]

The core hardening suffix -*'aḥs* 'being in a vessel' in (35) changes the stem-final fricative into *y̓*, whereas the peripheral hardening suffix -*'aƛ* TELIC in (36) does not.

---

[1] Sapir and Swadesh (Swadesh 1933; Sapir and Swadesh 1939) use the terms 'formative suffixes' and 'incremental suffixes' for these classes.

Core and peripheral suffixes also differ with respect to delabialization. When the stem ends with an underlyingly labialized consonant (rather than that resulting from labialization (see section 2.2.2), the labialization is lost before a peripheral suffix, but it is retained before a core suffix. Compare the following:

(37) *yaqii*
yaq^w ***-(y)i:***
one.who -INDF.3
'whoever'

(38) *yaaq*^{w}*iɬ*
yaq^w ***-(č)iɬ***
one.who -being.with.ref.to
'to whom'

In (37) attachment of a peripheral suffix *-(y)i:* INDEFINITE THIRD PERSON delabializes the underlying labialized consonant, whereas attachment of a core suffix *-(č)iɬ* 'being with reference to...' in (38) does not. Note that the delabialization phenomenon involving peripheral suffixes is reminiscent of delabialization at the word-final position. (See section 2.2.3).

Another difference in phonological effect between core and peripheral suffixes can be observed in the nature of change caused in the stem. Core suffixes can trigger changes that modify the core shape of the stem, such as lengthening and reduplication. In contrast, the change caused by peripheral suffixes is limited to the edge of a stem, i.e., hardening and softening.

The phonological facts described above suggest that core and peripheral suffixes belong to different phonological layers, with the former making the inner layer and the latter the outer layer of the word. This pattern is further confirmed by differences in other aspects of word-building.

In terms of the position within a suffix complex, core suffixes occur closer to the stem than peripheral suffixes.

Collocationally, core suffixes are much more constrained than are peripheral suffixes. A peripheral suffix can be attached to virtually any stem, while a core suffix strongly selects what it can be attached to.

Finally, core and peripheral suffixes differ also in terms of semantic scope. The scope of core suffixes is much more limited, typically a single stem or a syntactic complex formed on a single semantic head. The scope of most peripheral suffixes, on the other hand, covers a clause or a combination of clauses.

2.4.2. Core Suffixes

Included in the class of core suffixes are lexical suffixes and aspectual suffixes.

2.4.2.1. Lexical Suffixes

Nuuchahnulth has a large number (over 400) of suffixes with concrete lexical meanings. The range of meanings represented in the lexical suffixes is as wide as those of roots. The following is a sample list of lexical suffixes:

ACTIONS/EVENTS		STATES	
-ḥẇaɬ	'using ...'	*-yuˀa:ɬ*	'being aware of ...'
-'i·c	'eąting ...'	*-maḥsa*	'desiring to ...'
-ṅa:ḥ	'seeking ...'	*-ḥtin*	'being made of ...'
-ˀatu	'sinking into the water'	*-ḥta*	'being apart'

ENTITIES		LOCATIONS	
-ˀaq	'animal hide'	*-'is*	'being on the beach'
-mapt	'plant'	*-'as*	'being on the ground'
-qimɬ	'round object'	*-'a·*	'being on the rock'
-'aqsup	'female from ...'	*-'iɬ*	'being in the house'

Lexical suffixes must always be attached to some stem and can never stand alone. Most lexical suffixes do not have an etymologically related root form, but there are a very few pairs of lexical suffix and root that do share similar form and meaning, e.g., *wa·* 'say' and *-wa·* 'say; QUOTATIVE'. In most cases, however, the connection between such doublets is purely interpretive, and therefore it is not possible to speak of a systematic alternation between a root and a suffix in Nuuchahnulth.

A complex word formed with lexical suffixation may bear a surface resemblance to 'noun incorporation', mainly because both involve multiple lexical morphemes within a morphologically defined word. However, polysynthesis based on lexical suffixation and that based on noun incorporation should be clearly distinguished. With lexical suffixation, a word consists of a single root and suffixes that have lexical meanings, whereas noun incorporation is essentially a compounding of noun and verb roots (see Sapir 1911b: 251f.; Mithun 1984). In the following Nuuchahnulth examples, *ḥaaẇiiḥaƛ̓* 'boys' and *muut* 'boat' are roots, but *-(č)i:ɬ* 'making', *-yi:q* 'traveling on', and *-cuk* 'needing to' are suffixes because they cannot occur as, and are not etymologically related to, roots.

(39) *ḥaaw̓iiḥaƛiiɬʔaqƛʔick*
ḥa:w̓i:ḥaƛ -(č)i:ɬ -*ʔa·q(ƛ)* -*ʔick*
sons -making -FUT -IND.2sg

'You are going to have sons.' [CLLS 327]

(40) *muutyiiqcukʷit.*
mu:t -yi:q -*cuk* -*it*
boat -traveling.on -needing.to -PAST

'[In order to get there] we needed to take a boat.' [CLLS 221]

Unlike highly grammaticized derivational suffixes, like those in English, lexical suffixes in Nuuchahnulth have relatively concrete meanings. Consequently, the role these suffixes play in determining the semantic and syntactic characteristics of a word is more lexical than grammatical in nature: that is, the semantic contribution of each lexical suffix is highly idiosyncratic, and the effect on syntactic characteristics of the stem can be drastic. The functional roles that lexical suffixes play within word-building is discussed in detail in section 3.2.1.2.

When a lexical suffix is associated with a phrase[2] and has a semantic scope over it, attachment of the suffix follows a pattern that is rather unusual for a suffix: in most cases it is attached to the first constituent of the phrase regardless of the semantic head. This is illustrated in the set of examples below: the lexical suffix-*i:ɬ* 'making' is attached to the first constituent of a phrase regardless of its semantic head, i.e., *č̓apac* 'canoe'.

(41) *č̓aapaciiɬ*
č̓apac **-i:ɬ**
canoe -making

'He made a canoe.' [elicited GL]

(42) *ƛuɬiiɬ* *č̓apac*
ƛuɬ-i:ɬ *č̓apac*
nice-making canoe

'He made a nice canoe.' [elicited CL]

(43) *ʔiiḥiiɬ* *ƛuɬ* *č̓apac*
ʔi·ḥ **-i:ɬ** *ƛuɬ* *č̓apac*
greatly -making nice canoe

'He made a very nice canoe.' [elicited CL]

2 Note that the term 'phrase' is used here in a nontechnical, theory-neutral sense. It is intended to mean nothing more than 'a syntactically complex expression with some semantic unity'. The technical use of the term 'phrase' is introduced in section 4.2.2 with a specific structural definition. The technical and nontechnical uses of the term are indicated with the typeface: 'PHRASE' for the technical and 'phrase' for the nontechnical.

This 'suffix migration' phenomenon is observed only when the lexical suffix has a semantic scope over the phrase. Compare the lexical suffixes *-si:k* 'completing' and *-imɬ* 'all over' in the example below.

(44) *ˀiiḥsiiks* *ƛ̓isimɬ* *maḥɬii*
ˀi·ḥ ***-si:k*** *-s* *ƛ̓is* ***-imɬ*** *maḥɬi·*
large -completing -1sg white -all.over house
'He made a big white house.' [elicited CL]

Although both are lexical suffixes, only *-si:k* 'completing' shows the 'migration' behavior. The suffix *-imɬ* 'all over' only modifies *ƛ̓is* 'white' rather than the phrase as a whole, and therefore it retains its position regardless of the structure of the phrase.

Among lexical suffixes that can be associated with and have a semantic scope over a phrase, the nature of the scope relationship that they have with the target phrase is not homogeneous. One type of the scope phenomenon is observed with a lexical suffix expressing a verbal notion and a phrase expressing the notional object of the action or state expressed by the suffix. In (45) *-'inɬ* 'giving out, distributing' expresses a transitive notion and is associated with the expression that indicates the object of the action, i.e., the word *k̓acḥaq* 'blanket' in (45a) and the phrase *aya k̓acḥaq* 'many blankets' in (45b).

(45)

a. *k̓acḥaˤinɬit*
k̓acḥaq ***-'inɬ*** *-it*
blanket -distributing -PAST
'He gave out many blankets.' [GL 7.13.93-56]

b. *ˀayaˀinɬit* *k̓acḥaq*
ˀaya ***-'inɬ*** *-it* *k̓acḥaq*
many -distributing -PAST blanket
'He gave out many blankets.' [GL 7.13.93-60]

Examples in (46) further illustrate the same type of scope phenomenon.

(46)

a. *č̓apac̓uɬs*
č̓apac ***-'u·ɬ*** *-s*
canoe -owning -1sg
'I own a canoe [as means of transportation].' [GL 7.13.93-104]

b. *ˀiiw̓uuɬs* *č̓apac*
*ˀi:ḥʷ-**'u·ɬ*** *-s* *č̓apac*
large -owning -1sg canoe
'I own a big canoe [as means of transportation].' [GL 7.13.93-107]

Lexical suffixes that express locative notions can also exhibit 'suffix migration' when they are attached to a syntactically complex expression. The suffixes *-a·s* 'being on the surface' in (47) and *-čas* 'being at the crown' in (48) are placed on the first word in the phrase.

(47) *ˀaƛaasˀaƛukqun* *maƛimłm̓inḥ.*
ˀaƛa ***-a·s*** *-'aƛ -uk -qʷin* *maƛ -imł -m̓inḥ*
two -being.on.a.surface-TEL -POSS -COND.1pl tied -rounded.object -PL
we.placed.two.of.our barrels

'We used to put two barrels on the platform.' (lit. We used to have two barrels on the platform.) [CLLS 84]

(48) *ˀaƛačasqi* *ƛiḥuk* *ˁiyaał* *łuḥčiti,*
ˀaƛa ***-čas*** *-qi·* *ƛiḥ -uk* *ˁiya:ł* *łuḥčiti*
two -being.at.the.crown -being.on.top red -DUR feather head
two.at.the.crown.of.the.head red feather head

'There are two red feathers at the crown of his head.' [Canoe 13]

Another common case of 'suffix migration' involves lexical suffixes that semantically serve as a predicate with a clausal complement. For example, in (49) the suffix *-maḥsa* 'wanting to' semantically serves as a higher predicate that takes the complex expression *huuˀak̓at wałyaqpiˀat* 'one would go home early' as a complement, and it is attached to the first element rather than the second.

(49) *huuˀakmaḥsat* *wałyaqpiˀat*
hu:ˀak ***-maḥsa*** *-'at* *wał -yaq -'pi(ƛ) -'at*
early -wanting -SHIFT at.home -having.done -getting.in.the.house -SHIFT
'You would want to go home early.' [Canoe 93]

In the 'migration' phenomenon discussed above, lexical suffixes appear to shift their hosts. This suggests that placement of these lexical suffixes is determined in relation to the phrase as a whole rather than to the stem. Thus, the lexical suffix appears to attach mechanically on the first syntactic element within the phrase. Therefore one might argue that lexical suffixes are in fact clitics rather than suffixes. Superficially, this view seems to be reasonable and even attractive: it can readily provide an explanation for the unusual suffixation pattern. However, on closer examination the advantage of this view turns out not to be as definitive as it first appears. Typologically, it is rather odd for elements like lexical suffixes to be clitics. Clitics are typically found among the elements that are semantically and functionally external to word formation such as clause-level inflectional morphemes. Although a crosslinguistic definition of clitics has yet to be established uncontroversially, some characteristics have been recognized as common features of clitics. In addition to the 'migratory' placement pattern, clitics typically have the following characteristics (see Zwicky and Pullum 1983; Klavans 1985; Halpern 1992): (i) clitics do not show arbitrary gaps in the set of combinations; (ii) clitics do not trigger idiosyncratic morphological changes; (iii) the semantic contribution of clitics is highly regular and without idiosyncrasies; and (iv) positions of clitics are farther away from the root than those of suffixes. These four characteristics do not apply to lexical suffixes in Nuuchahnulth.

First, lexical suffixes show a high degree of selection restriction that is similar to that of independent lexical items, and consequently the range of possible combinations is highly restricted and is full of arbitrary gaps. (See section 3.2.1.2.) For example, *-i·c* 'consuming food' can only be combined with an expression that indicates a food item (see 50), *-ḥw̓ał* 'using' only with an instrument (see 51).

(50) *muk̓ʷiic*
muk **-'i·c**
deer -eating
'eat deer' [7.24.91-83]

(51) *č̓iimḥw̓ał*
č̓i:m **-ḥw̓ał**
knife -using
'use a knife' [7.24.91-60]

Considering the lexical nature of their meaning, it is not surprising for lexical suffixes to show such combinatorial idiosyncrasies.

Second, unlike typical clitics, lexical suffixes can affect the internal structure of the word in a significant way, some of which can modify the core shape of the stem. (See section 2.4.1.) Examples (52) and (53) below show lexical suffixes that cause reduplication or lengthening in the stem.

(52) reduplication
a. ***suusuuw̓***iiḥ
su:ḥ -'i:ḥ
salmon -fishing.for
'fishing salmon' [7.21.94-37]

b. ***ƛuƛuq***yimł
ƛuq -yimł
wide -being.at.the.shoulder
'wide shoulder' [7.8.94-80]

(53) lengthening

a. ***čaapac̓ap***
čapac -'a·p
canoe -buying
'buy a canoe' [7.13.93-103]

b. ***wiikmiik***
wik -mi:k
nothing -getter.of
'a person that does not get anything [while hunting]' [7.13.93-80]

Lexical suffixes are also very different from clitics with respect to their semantic contribution. Being suffixes with lexical meanings, they contribute substantial and idiosyncratic meanings just as independent lexical items do.

The position of lexical suffixes in relation to other suffixes does not corroborate a view of lexical suffixes as clitics either. Lexical suffixes appear closer to the root than elements that are clearly suffixes, i.e., aspectual morphemes. In (54) and (55) lexical suffixes *-'i:ḥ* 'pursuing' and *-yu·k̓ʷaɬ* 'being absent' occur closer to the root *kamatq-* 'run' and *qii* 'long time', respectively, than the aspectual morpheme *-ši(ƛ)* MOMENTANEOUS.

(54) *kamatˁiiḥšiƛˀaaɬ*
kamatq ***-'i:ḥ*** ***-šiƛ*** *-ˀa:ɬ*
run -pursuing -MOM -always
'He always chases things around.' [Dog 3]

(55) *qiiyuuk̓ʷaɬšiˀaƛ*
qi: ***-yu·k̓ʷaɬ*** ***-ši(ƛ)*** *-'aƛ*
long.time -being.absent -MOM -TEL
'He has been gone for a long time.' [Mink 293]

Given that aspectual morphemes are semantically very closely tied to the root and never show 'migratory behavior', it is far-fetched to consider them 'clitics'. Thus, lexical suffixes must be thought of as occurring within the 'suffixation zone' rather than in the 'cliticization zone'. As long as we maintain the assumption that suffixation and cliticization belong to separate layers within word structure, with the former always occurring inside the latter, it is difficult to justify a view of lexical suffixes as clitics.

In sum, lexical suffixes in Nuuchahnulth are nothing like clitics that have been reported in different languages of the world, and therefore there is a serious burden of proof on the claim that lexical suffixes are, in fact, clitics. As we will see below, the structural evidence fails to provide inarguable support for the clitic analysis of lexical suffixes in Nuuchahnulth.

What motivates the clitic analysis of these morphemes is the low degree of selection with respect to the base of phonological dependence, as illustrated in the following set of examples.

(56)

a. *šuuwiiẏapˀiš*
šu:wis **-'a·p** *-ˀi·š*
shoes -buying -IND.3
'He bought shoes.' [CL 99.08.15-024]

b. *yacyułapˀiš* *šuuwis*
yacyut **-'a·p** *-ˀi·š* *šu:wis*
worn -buying -IND.3 shoes
'He bought used shoes.'

c. *ˀiiẇaapˀiš* *yacyut* *šuuwis*
ˀi:ḥʷ **-'a·p** *-ˀi·š* *yacyut* *šu:wis*
large -buying -IND.3 worn shoes
'He bought big used shoes.' [CL 99-08-15=028]

In the above examples it certainly appears that the lexical suffix floats over to the first element and does not have any inherent semantic and morphological selection relation with respect to the host. In other words, attachment of the lexical suffix does not appear to be governed by the meaning or morphological properties of the stem. However, in Nuuchahnulth, where lexical categories are highly indeterminate (see section 3.1), it is not certain that 'migratory' behavior in itself serves as evidence for the lack of a selection relation with respect to the stem properties. Specifically, stems that express meanings similar to those of English modifiers, such as *yacyut* 'used, worn' or *ˀi:ḥʷ* 'big', can be semantically and morphologically perfect hosts by themselves.

(57) *yacyułapˀiš*
yacyut **-'a·p** *-ˀi·š*
worn -buying -IND.3
'He bought a used one.'

(58) *ˀiiẇaapˀiš*
ˀi:ḥʷ **-'a·p** *-ˀi·š*
large -buying -IND.3
'He bought a big one.'

In other words, in Nuuchahnulth there is nothing unusual about having the lexical suffix *-'a·p* 'buying' attached to *yacyut* 'used, worn' or *ˀi:ḥʷ* 'big' to form a self-standing predicate. Thus, attachment of the suffix to the stems that do not seem to be the semantic head of the phrase does not necessarily prove a lack of selection relation between the lexical suffix and its hosts, and therefore it does not need to be explained as a result of the mechanical 'suffix migration' process.

As for the 'always-first' rule that seems to be at work in attachment of lexical suffixes, it could also be explained without relying on a clitic analysis. The order of modifying elements within the phrase is basically governed by the scope relationship: the stem that has a modificational scope over the other precedes the modified stem. (See 4.4.1.2 for further details.) For example, in (59) below the stem *ˀi:ḥʷ* 'very' has a modificational scope over *ƛuɬ* 'nice', and *ƛuɬ* in turn modifies the stem *maḥƛi·* 'house'.

(59) *ˀiiḥiiɬ* *ƛuɬ* *maḥƛii*
ˀi:ḥʷ-i:ɬ *ƛuɬ* *maḥƛi·*
very -making nice house
'He made a very nice house.' [CL]

At first glance, attachment of lexical suffixes appears to be sensitive to the position of the stem. However, since the order of stems is governed by the scope hierarchy, it is possible that the lexical suffixes are placed on the first stem because it is the modifier with the highest scope rather than because it physically occurs at the left-most position within the phrase. The 'always-first' attachment pattern, then, is a phenomenon that is triggered and governed by the semantic scope hierarchy within the phrase. In this view, attachment of lexical suffixes is fundamentally different in nature from that of clitics.

2.4.2.2. Aspect

An aspectual morpheme is an important part of word formation in that it deeply affects the semantic characteristics of a word, although not as specifically as a lexical suffix. An aspectual morpheme is not obligatory for every root. It is generally placed after lexical suffixes.

2.4.2.2.1. Momentaneous

The MOMENTANEOUS morpheme *-šiƛ* (*-kʷiƛ* following /u/, *-čiƛ* following other vowels; the final *ƛ* is deleted before hardening peripheral suffixes) typically expresses completion of an event or action.

(60)
a. *huḥtakšiƛ* 'recall' < *huḥtak* 'know'
b. *ƛiḥšiƛ* 'paddle away in a canoe' < *ƛiḥ-* 'travel in a canoe'
c. *čičiƛ* 'make a splash' < *či-* 'splash'
d. *watqšiƛ* 'swallow completely' < *watq-* 'swallow'
e. *sukʷiƛ* 'grab' < *su-* 'hold'
f. *łayuukʷiƛ* 'anchor' < *łayu:-* 'anchor'

A small number of roots take MOMENTANEOUS morphemes other than *-šiƛ*:

-u(ƛ) as in *m̓učičuƛ* 'get clothed' < *m̓učič-* 'clothed'
-in(ƛ) as in *mačinƛ* 'enter a house' < *mač-* 'enter a house'
-i(ƛ) as in *łačiƛ* 'let go' < *łač-* 'let go'

2.4.2.2.2. Durative

The DURATIVE morpheme has two allomorphs *-ak* (*-ˀak* following vowels) and *-uk*, whose distribution seems largely unpredictable. The DURATIVE typically expresses a nondynamic state.

(61)
a. *qaḥak* 'dead' < *qaḥ-* 'die'
b. *ƛiƛkak* 'muscular' < *ƛiƛk-* 'firm'
c. *ƛiḥuk* 'red' < *ƛiḥ-* 'red; being red'
d. *kinḥak* 'starving' < *kinḥ-* 'starve'

2.4.2.2.3. Continuative

The CONTINUATIVE morpheme *-(y)a·* (/y/ occurs after vowels) typically expresses continuation of a dynamic action or event.

(62)
a. *łapsaa* 'diving' < *łaps-* 'dive'
b. *č̓uyaa* '(fish) moving' < *č̓u-* '(fish) move'
c. *ḥaaḥuupa* 'teaching' < *ḥa:ḥu:p-* 'teach'
d. *piḥaa* 'examining' < *piḥ-* 'examine'

Although the above characterizations of DURATIVE and CONTINUATIVE may give the impression that uses of these two aspectual morphemes can be distinguished clearly, the distinction is unfortunately not as clean as one might hope.

(63) DURATIVE on continuation of a dynamic action

a. *kamatquk* < *kamatq-**uk*** 'running'

b. *ˤiḥak* < *ˤiḥ-**ak*** 'crying'

(64) CONTINUATIVE on a nondynamic state

a. *m̓iƛaa* < *m̓iƛ-**(y)a·*** 'raining'

b. *ƛupaa* < *ƛup-**(y)a·*** 'being warm'

2.4.2.2.4. Inceptive

The INCEPTIVE morpheme *-'i·čiƛ* expresses the inception of a state or event.

(65)

a. *kuˀiičiƛ* 'becoming daylight' < *ku-* 'daylight'

b. *ˤinm̓iičiƛ* 'becoming a snail' < *ˤinm̓i-* 'snail'

c. *ƛay̓uučiƛ* 'becoming fast' < *ƛay̓u-* 'fast'

d. *ƛaaqiičiƛ* 'starting to grow' < *ƛa:q-* 'grow'

e. *naˀiičiƛ* 'starting to hear' < *naˀa·* 'hear'

2.4.2.2.5. Iterative

There is a set of morphemes that express recurrence of an event or action at some intervals, which can be translated as 'every once in a while' or 'every now and then'. These morphemes seem to be in complementary distribution in relation to roots: that is, different morphemes seem to be associated with different sets of roots.

a. REDUP of root + ***-š*** (***-k*** after /*u*/; ***-č*** after other vowels)

waɬwaɬš 'go back home every once in a while' < *waɬ-* 'go home'

tastasš 'keep rubbing; rub every once in a while' < *tas-* 'rub'

b. ***-ši:ɬ*** [LENGTHENING]

huuḥtakšiiḥ 'keep learning' < *huḥtak* 'know'

c. ***-i:ł*** [LENGTHENING]
ˀaayaqsiił 'keep catching many' < *ˀaya-qs* 'catch many'

d. ***-'u:ł*** [LENGTHENING]
hiišumẏuuł 'gather every once in a while' < *hiš-umł* 'gather in a group'

2.4.2.2.6. Graduative

The GRADUATIVE morpheme is only realized as length in a root vowel and expresses the gradual progression of an event or action. The GRADUATIVE morpheme can co-occur with another aspect.

(66) *ƛiiḥšiƛ*
ƛiḥ -[L] *-ši(ƛ)*
travel.in.vessel -GRAD -MOM
'setting out in a canoe'

(67) *ˀaatḥšiƛ*
ˀatḥ -[L] *-ši(ƛ)*
night -GRAD -MOM
'becoming night'

(68) *čuušukʷiƛ.*
čuš -[L] *-uk* *-iƛ*
be.suspicious.of -GRAD -DUR -MOM
'starting to get suspicious'

2.4.2.2.7. Repetitive

The REPETITIVE morpheme *-(y)a* (/y/ occurs following vowels) is accompanied by reduplication of the whole root and GRADUATIVE aspect (i.e., lengthening effect on the root vowel). The REPETITIVE expresses regular repetition of an event or action.

(69)
a. *yaaxyaaxʷa* 'brushing repeatedly' < *yaxʷ-* 'brush'
b. *hiishiisa* 'chopping repeatedly' < *his-* 'chop'
c. *huułhuuła* 'dancing repeatedly' < *huł-* 'dance'
d. *yaackyaacka* 'kicking repeatedly' < *yack-* 'kick'

2.4.3. Peripheral Suffixes

Included in the class of peripheral suffixes are those expressing various modal concepts and person. Here I describe only peripheral suffixes that form a paradigm.

2.4.3.1. Person

Nuuchahnulth has a paradigmatic set of suffixes expressing the person value of the subject. The suffix is attached to the main predicate. The person suffix in Nuuchahnulth is pronominal, rather than an agreement marker, in that it can occur without a coreferential overt nominal.

(70) Person suffixes

	SINGULAR	PLURAL
1	*-s*	*-na*
2	*-su:k, -k*	*-su:*
3	Ø	Ø

For the third person, the plurality of the subject can be indicated with the suffix *-ˀa·ɬ*, but the use of this suffix is not obligatory.

The person suffixes take different shapes when they co-occur with 'mood' suffixes. However, it is rather difficult to determine the exact shape of the person suffixes in these cases, since many of the combinations of mood and person are inseparably fused. Thus, synchronically it seems appropriate to consider each mood as a paradigm with different forms for different persons. (See the next section.)

Person can be marked without mood, and in fact such isolated person marking is quite frequent. Consequently, the distribution of person marking is different from that of mood marking.

Person marking does not occur with predicates in a clause-chaining construction. (See the discussion of SERIALIZATION in section 4.4.2.1.) The majority of main predicates, however, is marked overtly for person either by a mood–person suffix or a person suffix alone. In a sample of two personal narratives in my database, over 90 percent of the main predicates in first person (247 out of 279) are marked for person.

2.4.3.2. Mood

There is a set of suffixes that have been called 'mood' suffixes in the literature (see Sapir and Swadesh 1939; Swadesh 1939; Rose 1981). Although the majority of the mood suffixes express modal concepts, the category of mood suffixes is not functionally homogeneous. The motivati on for treating these suffixes as a class lies instead in their behavioral characteristics. The suffixes belonging to the mood class are mostly in a paradigmatic relationship with each other and therefore cannot co-occur. In addition, mood suffixes are closely associated with the person suffixes, and in most cases mood and person suffixes are inseparably fused.

In this work I use the term 'mood suffix', following previous studies. I also follow the terminology that Sapir and Swadesh (1939) used to refer to the mood categories.

2.4.3.2.1. Indicative

The INDICATIVE mood is used for the assertion of facts. The INDICATIVE is by no means a default mood, and its use can add a strong assertive tone to a statement.

(71) Indicative suffixes

	SINGULAR	PLURAL
1	*-ˀi·š*	*-ni·š*
2	*-ˀick*	*-ˀicu:š*
3	*-ˀi·š*	*-ˀi·š*

(72) *wičšaḥapˀick,*
wič -šaḥap ***-ˀick***
wrong -acting -IND.2sg
'You are doing it in the wrong way.' [CLLS 172]

(73) *ˁinm̓iičiƛ̓ˀaqƛ̓ˀicuuš.*
ˁinm̓i -'i·či(ƛ̓) -ˀa·q(ƛ̓) ***-ˀicu:š***
snail -INC -FUT -IND.2pl
'You will become a snail.' [CLLS 183]

(74) *hiitkinˀiš ˁiniiƛ̓ˀi,*
hi:tkin ***-ˀi·š*** *ˁini:ƛ̓ -ˀi·*
strange -IND.3 dog -DEF
'The dog was strange.' [Dog 52]

2.4.3.2.2. Interrogative

The INTERROGATIVE mood is used in forming questions.

(75) Interrogative suffixes

	SINGULAR	PLURAL
1	*-ḥs*	*-ḥin*
2	*-ḥa·k*	*-ḥsu:*
3	*-ḥ*	*-ḥ*

(76) *waasiḥ*
wa:si ***-ḥ***
where -INTER.3

'Where is Kapchaa?' [Kingfisher 163]

(77) *ˀaqisḥitḥsuu šiiƛuk,*
ˀaqisḥ -it ***-ḥsu:*** *ši:ƛuk*
why -PAST -INTER.2p move

'Why did you move?' [CLLS 222]

(78) *waayaqpimitḥ ƛawaa town,*
wa:yaq -pi -mit ***-ḥ*** *ƛawa:*
which -being.most -PAST -INTER.3 near

'Which was the closest town?' [CLLS 219]

2.4.3.2.3. Quotative

The QUOTATIVE mood is used to indicate that an action, event, or state is reported by third parties and that the speaker does not have direct knowledge of it.

(79) Quotative suffixes

	SINGULAR	PLURAL
1	*-wa·ˀičas*	*-wa·ˀičin*
2	*-wa·ˀick*	*-wa·ˀicu:š*
3	*-wa·ˀiš*	*-wa·ˀiš*

(80) *waałšiƛwaˀick*
wał -[L] -*šiƛ* ***-wa·ˀick***
go.home -GRAD-MOM -QUOT.2sg
'[They say] you are going home.' [elicited CL]

(81) *hininwaˀiš* *qʷayaac̓ikm̓it,*
hin *-in* ***-wa·ˀi·š*** *qʷaya:c̓ik* *-m̓i·t*
get.there -coming -QUOT.3 wolf -son.of
'[They say] the Son of Wolf came.' [Mink 60]

(82) *tiičmaḥsamitwaˀiš* *c̓awaak.*
ti:č-maḥsa *-'ap* *-it* ***-wa·ˀi·š*** *c̓awa:k*
live -wanting.to -CAUS -PAST -QUOT.3 one
'[They say] one [of the warriors] wanted to save his life.' [Kingfisher 251]

2.4.3.2.4. Conditional

The CONDITIONAL mood expresses counterfactuality and habitual (temporally non-specific) action.

(83) Conditional suffixes

	SINGULAR	PLURAL
1	*-qu:s*	*-qʷin*
2	*-qu:k*	*-qu:su:*
3	*-qu:*	*-qu:*

(84) Counterfactual / Hypothetical

a. *ˀumaak* *ˀaḥ* *p̓ussiƛquu,* *tuxwiiḥaquu,*
ˀuma:k *ˀaḥ* *p̓us* *-ši(ƛ)****-qu:*** *tuxwi:ḥa* ***-qu:***
because.of he tired -MOM -COND.3 get.out.of.breath -COND.3
it.is.because.of he would.get.tired would.get.out.of.breath

'[He didn't eat too much] because [if he did] he would get tired and out of breath.' [Wolf 73]

b. *wik̓atquu* *ˁačuuˀat.*
wik-'at ***-qu:*** *ˁaču:* *-'at*
not -SHIFT -COND.3 wounded -SHIFT
may.there.be.none one.gets.wounded

'May there be no wounds.' [Canoe 7]

(85) Habitual

a. *č̓itkˀisˀiš* *waaˀaƛquu* *n̓uw̓iiqsakitqs.*
č̓itkˀis -ˀi·š *wa: -'aƛ-**qu:*** *n̓uw̓i:qsu -ak -it -qs*
easily.cut -IND.3 say -TEL-COND.3 father -POSS-PAST-SUB.1sg
cut.easily he.used.to.say my.father

'My father used to say "it is soft [easily cut]".' [Canoe 142]

b. *ˀucačiˀaƛqʷin* *ḥuu* *hiłstiisˀi,*
*ˀu -ca -či(ƛ)-'aƛ -**qʷin*** *ḥu:* *hił -sti·s -ˀi·*
it -going.to -MOM -TEL -COND.1pl yonder be.there-moving.into.the.interior -DEF
we.would.go.to.it yonder upper.interior

'We used to go way up into the inlet.' [CLLS 29]

The CONDITIONAL mood can also be used to express a conditional notion that could be translated as 'if/when' in English.

(86) Conditional

a. *ƛiiḥcuutˀaał,*
ƛi:ḥ -cu:t -ˀa:ł
move.pointwise -being.on...side -always

wik̓aƛquu *čačamḥi* *sipuus.*
*wik-'aƛ **-qu:*** *čačam-ḥi·* *sipu:s*
not -TEL -COND.3 proper -DUR keel

'It [canoe] always veers to one side if the keel is not properly set.' [Canoe 44]

b. *qʷiyuqʷin* *č̓aapaciił* *ˀuuḥw̓ałckʷi* *ˀiščiip* *huuˀak.*
*qʷiyu **-qʷin*** *č̓apac -i:ł* *ˀu -ḥw̓ał -ckʷi·* *ˀišči:p* *hu:ˀak*
when -COND.1pl canoe -making it -using -having.happened pitch long.ago
when.we.were making.a.canoe having.used.it pitch long.ago

'A long time ago, when we were making a canoe, we used pitch.' [Canoe 186]

2.4.3.2.5. Dubitative

The DUBITATIVE mood is used to express the speaker's uncertainty about the truthfulness of the statement.

(87) Conditional suffixes

	SINGULAR	PLURAL
1	*-qa·ca*	*-qa·č̓ina*
2	*-qa·čka*	*-qa·cu:wa*
3	*-qa·č̓a*	*-qa·č̓a*

(88) *ʔaƛ̓pupititqač̓a*
ʔaƛ̓pu -p̓it -it ***-qa·č̓a***
seven -times -PAST -DUB.3

'It might have happened seven times.' [Canoe 156]

(89) *tiičsyumčqač̓a.*
ti:č -syumč ***-qa·č̓a***
life -asing.for -DUB.3

'I guess he was asking for well-being.' [Little's-I 89]

2.4.3.2.6. Purposive

The PURPOSIVE mood expresses the purpose or aim of another action.

(90) Purposive suffixes

	SINGULAR	PLURAL
1	*-'a:ḥ*	*-'a:ni*
2	*-'a:ʔick*	*-'a:ʔicu:*
3	*-'a:ʔit*	*-'a:ʔit*

(91) *maƛ̓šiʔi* *šuuwisukʔitk,*
maƛ̓ -ši(ƛ̓)-'i· *šu:wis -uk -ʔitk*
tie -MOM -IMP.2s>3 shoes -POSS-REL.2
tie.it your.shoes

wik̓aaʔick *hiixtaq.*
wik ***-'a:ʔick*** *hi:xtaq*
not -PURP.2sg have.accident
so.as.not.for.you.to have.accident

'Tie your shoe laces so you won't have an accident.' [elicited 07.03.91-037]

(92) *ˀuḥ pihpiḥšiˀat,*
ˀuḥ REDUP-*piḥ* *-ši(ƛ)-'at*
be.it ITER- examining -MOM -SHIFT
be.it it.is.examined

wik̓aaˀit *cicikpała.*
*wik-***'a:ˀit** DUP-*cik* *-pała*
not -PURP.3 aslant -being.on.each.side
so.that.it.will.not.be aslant.on.both.side

'Take a good look at it so it will not be out of alignment.' [Canoe 43]

2.4.3.2.7. Subordinate

The SUBORDINATE mood appears to be used to indicate an irrealis complement. However, in the present corpus the number of occurrences of this suffix is very limited, and its function cannot be determined precisely at this point.

(93) Subordinate suffixes

	SINGULAR	PLURAL
1	*-qs*	*-qin*
2	*-k*	*-qsu:*
3	*-q*	*-q*

(94) *ˀuqłaapckʷi* *qaḥsaapw̓iłasˀatq,*
ˀuqła:p -ckʷi· *qaḥ -sa·p -w̓iłas -'at* ***-q***
believe -having.done dead -MOMCAUS -about.to -SHIFT -SUB.3
thought they.are.going.to.kill.him

'He thought that they were going to kill him.' [Kingfisher 236]

(95) *ˀuqłaap̓aƛ* *qʷayac̓iik,* *takaatisˀaqƛq.*
ˀuqła:p -'aƛ *qʷayac̓i:k* *tak -a:t -'is -ˀa·qƛ* ***-q***
think -TEL wolf head.to -moving.downstream -being.on.the.shore -FUT -SUB.3
thought wolf will.go.down.the.stream

'Wolves thought that the mink would go down the stream of the current.' [Mink 144]

2.4.3.2.8. Relative

The RELATIVE mood suffix is used to nominalize a predicate.

(96) Relative suffixes

	SINGULAR	PLURAL
1	*-qs*	*-qin*
2	*-ˀi·tk*	*-ˀitqsu:*
3	*-ˀi·tq*	*-ˀi·tq*

(97)

ˀuuktisˀaƛ̓atˀiš	*q̓ʷaaxtii,*	*hisiikˀitq*
ˀu -ktis -'aƛ̓ -'at -ˀi·š	*q̓ʷa:xti:,*	*his -i·k* ***-ˀi·tq***
it -acting.by.ref.to -TEL -SHIFT -IND.3	NAME	get.there -going.along -REL.3
they.are.following.it	NAME	path.he.took

'They were following Qwaaxtii's path.' [Mink 168]

(98)

ˀiiqḥukʷaƛ̓	*qʷisitˀitq,*
ˀi:qḥ -uk -'aƛ̓	*qʷis -it* ***-ˀi·tq***
tell -DUR -TEL	do.so -PAST -REL.3
told	what.he.went.through

'He told what he went through.' [Qawiqaalth 154]

(99)

piḥšiˀat	*qʷaaˀasˀitq*
piḥ -ši(ƛ̓)-'at	*qʷa: -'as* ***-ˀi·tq***
examine -MOM -SHIFT	thus -being.on.the.ground -REL.3
examine	the.way.it.is.on.the.ground

'Look over the way it is on the ground.' [Canoe 21]

(100)

kačiˀat	*ˀuunamaḥsap̓atˀitq*	*č̓apac,*
ka -či(ƛ̓)-'at	*ˀu:na -maḥsa -'ap -'at* ***-ˀi·tq***	*č̓apac*
measure -MOM -SHIFT	size -wanting.to -CAUS -SHIFT -REL.3	canoe
measure	how.long.it.is.wanted.to.be	canoe

'Measure for the length you want the canoe to be.' [Canoe 22]

2.4.3.2.9. Indefinite Relative

The INDEFINITE RELATIVE mood nominalizes a predicate with the implication that there is an uncertainty or indeterminacy associated with that predicate.

(101) Indefinite Relative suffixes

	SINGULAR	PLURAL
1	*-(y)i:s*	*-(y)in*
2	*-(y)i:k*	*-(y)i:su:*
3	*-(y)i:*	*-(y)i:*

(102) *haʔukšiƛ quum̓iiʔanitii.*
haʔuk -ši(ƛ) qu:m̓a -'i·(ƛ) -'at -it ***-(y)i:***
eat -MOM how.many -inviting-SHIFT -PAST -INDF.3
ate how.many.that.might.have.been.invited

'However many people that were invited [all of the people that were invited] ate.' [Qawiqaalth 186]

(103) *hayimḥiniš hiɬii*
hayim -ḥi· -ni·š hiɬ ***-(y)i:***
not.know -DUR -IND.1pl be.there -INDF.3
we.don't.know wherever.he.would.be

'We don't know where he would be.' [Kingfisher 164]

The INDEFINITE RELATIVE mood is also commonly used to express indeterminacy or uncertainty in a non-nominalized predicate.

(104) *ʔinumsaqk̓ukʷina n̓iƛaak.*
ʔinums -aq -k̓uk ***-(y)ina*** *n̓iƛa:k*
seldom -very -apparently -INDF.1pl fighting
it.seems.like.we.would.rarely fighting

'It seems that we rarely quarreled.' [CLLS 189]

(105) *waamitii.*
wa· -mit ***-(y)i:***
say -PAST -INDF.3

'He might have said so.' [Mink 151]

(106) *qʷiʔiimitii*
qʷi -ʔi: -mit ***-(y)i:***
that.which -get.to.be.at -PAST -INDF.3

'He went to some place.' [Mink 207]

2.4.3.2.10. Imperative

The IMPERATIVE mood is used to make a command or hortative expression. The IMPERATIVE is unique in that it occurs only with the first- or second-person subject and also in that it is the only mood occurring with a suffix indicating the object.

(107) Imperative suffixes

		OBJECT		
		1S	1P	3
SUBJECT	2S	*-'i·s*	*-'in*	*-'i·*
	2P	*-'i·čas*	*-'i·čin*	*-'i·č*
	1P	—	—	*-'in*

(108) *ˁuyaasaƛin*
*ˁuya:s -'aƛ-***'in**
move -TEL -IMP.1p
let's.move

'Let's move [to some other place].' [GLLS 134]

(109) *kuḥsaap̓ič.*
kuḥ -sa·p **-'i·č**
open -MOMCAUS -IMP.2p>3s

'You all make an opening.' [Mink 110]

(110) *tiič̓ap̓is,*
ti:č -'ap **-'i·s**
be.alive -CAUS -IMP.2s>1s

'Let me live.' [Mink 260]

(111) *naaˀuuqstaˀičin*
naˀu· -'a·qsta **-'i·čin**
accompany -being.amongst -IMP.2p>1p

'Join us.' [CLLS 269]

2.4.3.2.11. Placement of Mood Suffixes

Overt marking of mood is not obligatory. The form without overt mood marking has been called the 'absolutive form' (Sapir 1924; Swadesh 1939) and has been characterized as 'used in narrative when the mode [= mood] has already been indicated in a previous sentence' (Swadesh 1939: 82). This treatment of the mood-less form may suggest that it is a structurally dependent elliptical form with a limited, highly specific distribution. This, however, is too much of an idealization. In actual discourse a majority of sentences have the main predicate in the absolutive form, lacking overt mood marking. For example, in a narrative text of about 310 sentences, only 19 percent (59 out of 310) of the main predicates are marked with mood suffixes.

Within the word, mood suffixes always follow core suffixes. This is more or less expected given the inflection-like functions of the mood suffixes.

When mood suffixes are associated with a syntactically complex expression, i.e., phrase, they are attached to the element that comes at the beginning of the expression. (For a similar phenomenon involving lexical suffixes, see section 2.4.2.1.)

(112)

a. *ḥaw̓iƛ̓ʔiš.*
ḥaw̓ił ***-ʔi·š***
chief -IND.3
'He is a chief.'

b. *ƛ̓ułʔiiš ḥaw̓ił.*
ƛ̓uł ***-ʔi·š*** *ḥaw̓ił*
good -IND.3 chief
'He is a good chief.'

c. *ʔiiḥʔiš ƛ̓uł ḥaw̓ił.*
ʔi·ḥ ***-ʔi·š*** *ƛ̓uł ḥaw̓ił*
really -IND.3 good chief
'He is a really good chief.'

When there is flexibility in the order among modifying elements within the complex expression, such as *ʔaani* 'really' illustrated below, mood suffixes attach to the stem that occupies the initial position.

(113)

a. ***ʔaaniʔiš*** *ƛ̓uł ḥaw̓ił.*
ʔa:ni ***-ʔi·š*** *ƛ̓uł ḥaw̓ił*
really -IND.3 good chief
'He is a really good chief.'

b. *ƛ̓ułʔiiš* ***ʔaani*** *ḥaw̓ił.*
*ƛ̓ułʔ**-i·š*** *ʔa:ni ḥaw̓ił*
good -IND.3 really chief
'He is a really good chief.'

Such dynamism in placement of mood suffixes suggests that the position of mood suffixes is not governed by the inherent properties of the stem serving as a host, but that it is instead determined dynamically based on the configuration of the stems within the complex expression.

Mood suffixes can be associated with various types of syntactically complex expressions, but they seem to be attached consistently to the first stem rather than the perceived semantic head within the complex. The following examples illustrate the attachment pattern within a nominal phrase. For example, in (114) the mood suffix *-ˀi·š* INDICATIVE THIRD PERSON is attached to the first stem expressing the property concept *p̓išaq* 'be bad' rather than the stem *ˀiiqḥy̓ak* 'news, story' which is the semantic head of the syntactic complex. The suffix FUTURE IMPERATIVE SECOND SINGULAR in (115) follows the same pattern.

(114) property concept + nominal

p̓išaqˀiš	*ˀiiqḥy̓ak.*
p̓išaq ***-ˀi·š***	*ˀi:qḥ -y̓akʷ*
be.bad-IND.3	telling -instrument

'There is bad news.' [Kingfisher 98]

ˀiiwačiˀim	*čaˀak.*
*ˀi:ḥʷ-'ači(ƛ)****-'i·m***	*čaˀak*
big -INC -IMP.2s.FUT	river

'You become a large river!' (used to cast a magic spell) [Mink 160]

(115) qualifier + nominal

ˀiiqḥiiˀiš	*čačumḥi*	*ḥaw̓ił*
ˀi:q-ḥi· ***-ˀi·š***	*čačum-ḥi·*	*ḥaw̓ił*
still -DUR -IND.3	proper -DUR	chief

'He is still an honorable chief.' [CL]

Mood suffixes are placed in the same way with respect to complex expressions of a verbal kind.

(116)

ˀiiḥinaˀaał	*qii*	*hił*	*ˁaqwitis.*
ˀi:ḥʷ ***-(y)ina*** *-ˀa:ł*	*qi:*	*hił*	*ˁaqwitis*
greatly -INDF.1pl -always	for.long	be.there	NAME

'We stayed in Aqwitis for a long time.' [CL30]

(117)

ˀiiḥwaˀiš	*taˀił*
*ˀi:ḥʷ****-wa·ˀiš***	*taˀił*
very QUOT.3	sick

'He is very sick.' [GL 7.8.94-84]

The attachment pattern that selects the initial stem over the semantic head also holds with respect to an expression consisting of multiple clauses. (See section 4.4.2.1.3 for a related discussion on the structural relationship between clauses in a predication.) In the following examples, the CONDITIONAL suffix is attached to the first predicate.

(118) *huuʔakʔaƛquus* *mamuuk.*
hu:ʔak-'aƛ ***-qu:s*** *mamu:k*
early -TEL -COND.1sg work
'I would work early.' [GLLS 147]

(119) *kʷiscačiʔaƛquu* *šiiƛuk.*
kʷis -ca -či(ƛ)-'aƛ ***-qu:*** *ši:ƛuk*
different -going.to -MOM -TEL -COND.3 move
would.go.to.different.places move
'He used to move around to different places.' [CKI 93]

The 'migration' phenomenon involving placement of mood suffixes, just like that of lexical suffixes, is strongly reminiscent of the behavior of clitics, which inevitably raises the suspicion that mood suffixes are in fact clitics.

Compared to the situation involving lexical suffixes, the clitic analysis is much more reasonable (that is, typologically plausible) for mood suffixes. Mood suffixes have the properties that are typically found in clitics in languages of the world. Specifically, they (i) do not show arbitrary gaps in the set of combinations, (ii) do not morphophonologically affect the stem drastically (compared to derivational elements), (iii) make a highly regular semantic contribution, and (iv) occur relatively far away from the stem (compared to derivational elements).

Nevertheless, analysis of mood suffixes in Nuuchahnulth as clitics is not as obvious or plausible as it at first appears. The problem is that the attachment of mood suffixes in Nuuchahnulth is not as mechanical as that of clitics. Typically, placement of clitics is not governed by or sensitive to the semantic or morphological properties of the host. Placement of mood suffixes in Nuuchahnulth, however, is clearly sensitive to the grammatical properties of the stem: these suffixes can never be attached to nonpredicative elements within the syntactic complex. For example, in (120) the nonpredicative stem *Helen* occurs as the first element within the syntactic complex that the mood suffix *-qu:s* is associated with.

(120) ***Helen*** *ˀukčumyiłˀaƛquus*

ˀu -(k)či -umł -'ił -'*aƛ* ***-qu:s***

it -being.along.with -being.in.a.group -beng.in.the.house -TEL -COND.1sg

I.would.be.on.the.floor.with.her

huułhuuła.

REDUP: *-huł -a*

ITER -dance -REP

dancing

'Helen and I would be out on the floor dancing.' [CLLS 175]

Here the mood suffix is found on the second stem, which is predicative, rather than on the first stem. Another example is seen in (121):

(121) ***ˀaˀiiḥ***	***nuučyuu***	*qacqasaƛquuč*	*ˀuušyuuya.*
ˀaˀi:ḥʷ	*nu:čyu:*	*qacqas* -'*aƛ* ***-qu:*** ***-č***	*ˀu:š -yu:ya*
large	mountain.range	disappear -TEL -COND.3 -INF	some -at.the.time
large	mountain.range	would.disappear	sometimes

'Sometimes [sea lions would go away from their home where there are large mountains — so far that] the large mountains would become out of sight.' [Qawiqaalth 106]

In this example *ˀaˀiiḥ nuučyuu* forms a complex that serves as an argument to the main predicate *qacqasaƛ*, and therefore it is nonpredicative. And again, the mood suffixes *-qu:* and *-č* are attached to the predicative stem, even though it is not initial. It is clear that mood suffixes in Nuuchahnulth can only be attached to predicative stems. Mood suffixes in Nuuchahnulth are in fact attached to the first predicative stem instead of to any first element within the complex. Thus, the placement of mood suffixes in Nuuchahnulth is not as free from grammatical selection restrictions as that of typical clitics.

There still remains the question of why mood suffixes 'migrate' to the first predicative stem. Just as I argued with respect to the clitic-like placement of lexical suffixes, the 'migration' of mood suffixes can be considered to be triggered and governed by the semantic scope hierarchy among the elements within the complex: mood suffixes are attached to the stem that is at the top of the scope hierarchy within the complex. This analysis has the advantage over a clitic analysis in that it does not require a separate ad hoc explanation about why nonpredicative stems are ignored in determining the 'first stem'.

Given the fact that there is some degree of grammatical selection with respect to the stem, and also the fact that there is an alternative account for the 'migration' phenomenon, it seems reasonable to conclude that mood elements in Nuuchahnulth are a special type of suffix. The domain of their attachment can be syntactically complex, and the position of attachment is governed by semantic organization, i.e., the scope hierarchy, within the complex.

2.4.3.2.12. The Nature of Mood Suffixes

Mood suffixes show characteristics of 'inflection': (i) they always follow derivational suffixes (lexical, causative, and PERSPECTIVE-SHIFTING suffixes), (ii) they can be attached to any predicate regardless of its semantic properties, (iii) their meanings/functions are highly abstract or grammaticized, and (iv) they form paradigmatic sets. But, unlike typical inflectional suffixes, they are not structurally obligatory. Although there is variation in the degree of obligatoriness, these suffixes are not required in the sense that the lack of such a suffix automatically leads to an ungrammatical form or to an interpretation as a 'zero' marking of some constant value. Thus, to the extent that structural obligatoriness is a defining characteristic of inflectional suffixes crosslinguistically, it is doubtful that one should call the mood suffixes in Nuuchahnulth 'inflectional'. This issue, however, is extrinsic to the internal organization of Nuuchahnulth grammar.

3

THE NATURE OF WORD CLASSES AND WORD FORMATION

Word-level structure in Nuuchahnulth is typologically rather unusual, which has important implications for the uniqueness of the language on the syntax level. This chapter discusses the nature of word classes and word formation in light of implications for syntactic patterning. It lays out the structural environment in which the syntactic patterning identified in the following chapter can be situated, thereby providing a better understanding of the syntax, especially with regard to the functional and structural motivations behind it.

3.1. Word Classes

Most words in Nuuchahnulth are inflectable.[1] Words that do not take inflectional suffixes include proper names, demonstratives, interjections, and some conjunctions.

In Nuuchahnulth, inflectable words, whether morphologically simple or complex, are syntactically very versatile, and therefore it is difficult to identify word classes based on the range of syntactic functions they can serve. However, this does not necessarily mean that words in Nuuchahnulth are completely homogeneous. On the contrary, there are some notable variations in functional and distributional propensities among words. I seek to explain how this heterogeneity relates to word classes and what the nature of such word classes is.

3.1.1. Previous Studies

In Nuuchahnulth, all inflectable stems, regardless of their perceived semantic differences, are potentially predicative. Therefore it is difficult to distinguish different lexical

[1] Sapir and Swadesh (Sapir and Swadesh 1939; Swadesh 1939) use the terms 'normal words' and 'particles' for inflectable and noninflectable words, respectively.

categories on the basis of the inherent grammatical properties of stems. Facing this difficulty, Sapir and Swadesh (Sapir and Swadesh 1939; Swadesh 1939) take the position that inflectable stems cannot be subdivided into lexical categories. Swadesh (1939: 78) summarizes this view as follows:

> Normal words [= inflectable stems] do not fall into classes like noun, verb, adjective, preposition, but all sorts of ideas find their expression in the same general type of word, which is predicative or non-predicative according to its paradigmatic ending. The same word can be used now as the nucleus of the predication, now as a subsidiary element in the predication by the mere adding or dropping (or changing) of the modal ending.

Sapir and Swadesh's caution against allowing the imposition of traditional lexical categories as established within European linguistics was appropriate, especially at a time when awareness of typological variability was still relatively low in the linguistic community as a whole. However, as Jacobsen (1979a) points out, the above statement exaggerates the situation to the extent that it suggests that the functional and distributional propensities of stems in Nuuchahnulth are indistinguishable. All of these stems do not have homogeneous behavioral characteristics: not all stems are equally likely to serve a certain syntactic function or to occur in a certain syntactic context.

Researchers, including Sapir and Swadesh themselves, have been aware of the heterogeneous functional and distributional propensities of inflectable stems, but they differ in their evaluation of the nature of possible structural classes. Swadesh (1939) and Rose (1981) relate the behavioral variation among stems to semantic classes, treating it as an epiphenomenon stemming from the inherent semantic values of stems. Jacobsen (1979a), on the other hand, considers the behavioral variation to be grammatical in nature, linking it to lexical categories.

3.1.1.1. Semantic Approaches

Both Swadesh (1939) and Rose (1981) try to capture behavioral heterogeneity in terms of semantically defined classes, although the two differ in the way they formulate the classes. Swadesh (1939: 99f.) posits seven semantic classes: ENTITY, STATE, ACTION, LOCATION, TIME, QUANTITY, and INDICATION. These classes are based on meanings represented in a set of seven 'special reference stems', roots with anaphoric or cataphoric semantic qualities, including *ˀu-* 'it', *qʷa-* 'be thus, such', *qʷis* 'do thus', *hiɬ* 'be at that place', *ˀuyi* 'be at that time', *ˀana-* 'be thus much, thus many', and *ˀaḥˀaa* 'that (one)'. Rose's semantic classes include VERBAL, ADJECTIVAL, NOMINAL, LOCATIVE, QUANTIFIER,

QUANTITY, and TEMPORAL, and seem to be defined in purely semantic terms, although Rose (1981: 344f.) mentions some grammatical correlates of these classes.

There are problems inherent in meaning-based approaches that make them less useful in describing behavioral heterogeneity among stems. First, it is very difficult to determine in a nonarbitrary way the most appropriate set of classes purely on the basis of semantic values of stems. Rose's semantic classes seem reasonable, but there is no easy way to evaluate the appropriateness of the proposed scheme in Nuuchahnulth. Swadesh's semantic classes appear less arbitrary in that they are based on semantic distinctions represented in the lexicon, but even here it is not obvious whether the distinctions represented in the set of 'special reference stems' provide a good framework for the description of the structuring patterns in Nuuchahnulth. Furthermore, it is difficult to determine the inherent semantic value, and consequently class membership, of lexical items or expressions. Especially in a language like Nuuchahnulth, where stems are functionally versatile, it is very difficult to determine in a consistent, nonarbitrary way the inherent semantic value of a lexical item or expression.

Thus, although the meanings of stems are certainly useful in explaining various behavioral patterns, approaches to lexical categories based on lexically inherent semantic values do not provide a fully satisfactory account of general structural patterning.

3.1.1.2. A Structural Approach

Jacobsen (1979a), in his careful study of the problem of lexical categories, argues that behavioral heterogeneity provides a basis for distinguishing different lexical categories in Nootkan languages, directly challenging Sapir and Swadesh's statement about the lack of lexical categories in Nuuchahnulth.

In Nuuchahnulth it is possible to differentiate types of syntactic relationship and function in relation to different syntactic constructions. (See sections 4.1 and 4.2.) With respect to a given type of syntactic relationship, stems in the language are not equal in terms of how and how often they enter the relationship. Jacobsen makes an important contribution in explicitly recognizing this functional and behavioral heterogeneity among stems.

Based on the functional and distributional propensities of words (that is, potentiality of participation in different types of syntactic constructions), Jacobsen proceeds to distinguish six different lexical categories ('parts of speech' or 'word classes') in Nootkan: verbs, nouns, adjectives, adverbs, auxiliary verbs, and prepositions.[2] The proposed classes generally seem reasonable and useful for thinking about how word-level structure ties in with the larger syntactic structuring in Nuuchahnulth.

---

[2] Jacobsen's proposal is made on the basis of facts and data from Makah, but for the most part his proposal is applicable to Nuuchahnulth without significant modification.

3.1.2. Word Classes in Nuuchahnulth

Inflectable words in Nuuchahnulth are not homogeneous in terms of how they participate in different types of syntactic constructions, and there is some consistent association between sets of words and syntactic functions (configurational roles). These two statements do not contradict Sapir and Swadesh's (1939) view that it is not possible to divide inflectable Nootkan words into mutually exclusive categories. As is elaborated below, the word classes proposed here do not represent highly specialized, mutually exclusive lexical categories like those found in English.

3.1.2.1. Nominals and Verbals

I find one division among inflectable words in Nuuchahnulth to be fairly solid and of far-reaching structural relevance, i.e., NOMINALS vs. VERBALS. Semantically, nominals usually designate entities, while verbals typically express dynamic, relational, and attributive concepts. There are three kinds of behavioral differences that motivate the identification of these classes.

First, words have a tendency to be used either as referring expressions or as predicating expressions and can be used only in a limited way for the nonpreferred function. Nominal words like *c̓apac* 'canoe', *maḥt̓ii* 'house', and *qʷayac̓iik* 'wolf' are much more likely to be used as referring expressions, and when they are presented in isolation, they are most likely to be interpreted as expressions referring to objects or referable concepts. This functional skewing is reflected structurally by the fact that nominals are more likely to serve as arguments than as predicates. Although a nominal can be used by itself as a predicate, a nominal predicate is always inherently durative and can only make an existential, classifying, or identifying expression.

(122) Existential

a. *yuupickʷimatak*
yu:pi -ckʷi· *-matak*
breeze-having.happened -probably
'Probably there was a breeze.' [Kingfisher 3]

b. *c̓apacisˀiš*
c̓apac -'is *-ˀi·š*
canoe -being.on.the.beach -IND.3
'There is a canoe on the beach.' [elicited CL]

(123) Classifying

a. *ḥaaḥuupač̓ak*

ḥa:ḥu:p	*-(y)a*	*-č̓ak*
instructing	-CONT	-instrument

'This is a teaching.' [Canoe 16]

b. *ḥaaw̓iłaƛ̓aƛ qaaḥma*

ḥa:w̓iłaƛ̓-'aƛ	
young.man-TEL	NAME

'Qaahma was a young man.' [Kingfisher 121]

(124) Identifying

a. *čims*

čims

bear

'It was a bear.' [Mink 56]

b. *ḥawiłimmatak*

ḥawił	*-im*	*-matak*
chief	-thing	-probably

'It was probably the pack leader [of the wolves].' [Mink 87]

On the other hand, verbals such as *waˀič* 'sleep', *sukʷiƛ* 'take', and *naˀaa* 'hear' function predicatively by default. Generally they cannot directly serve as arguments.

Second, there is an operation that changes the adaptability to discourse function, i.e., nominalization for verbals. As indicated above, verbals generally cannot occur as arguments. This inherent limitation, however, can be overcome through nominalization with the use of *-ˀi·* DEFINITE. Compare the direct and nominalized uses of verbals *siqiił*, *haaˀumtaḥ*, and *ˀinksy̓iqiił* in the following example.

(125)

siqiił		***siqiiłˀi,***			*haaˀumtaḥ*		***haaˀumtaḥˀi,***		
siq	*-i:ł*	*siq*	*-i:ł*	***-ˀi·***	*haˀum-taḥ*		*haˀum-taḥ*		***-ˀi·***
cooked	-making	cooked	-making	-DEF	food	-gathering	food	-gathering	-DEF
cook		one.who.cooks			go.out.for.food		one.who.gathers.food		

waa	*ˀinksy̓iqiił*		***ˀinksy̓iqiiłˀi.***		
wa·	*ˀinksy̓iq*	*-i:ł*	*ˀinksy̓iq*	*-i:ł*	***-ˀi·***
and	firewood	-making	firewood	-making	-DEF
and	make.firewood		one.who.makes.firewood		

'The person in charge of cooking cooked, the one in charge of gathering food went out to gather food, and the one in charge of making firewood made it.' [CLLS 10]

Third, when words are modified (for MODIFICATION see sections 4.4.1.2 and 4.4.2.2), they are associated with a limited range of modifying expressions, and the pattern of combinatorial possibilities is not random. Nominals can be modified with expressions of property concepts, quantity, or quantifiers, but not directly with qualifying expressions like *hiikʷaɬ* 'almost' or *ˀanaƛuu* 'barely'.

(126) Property concept modifying nominal

a. *ƛuɬ č̓apac*
ƛuɬ č̓apac
nice canoe
'a nice canoe'

b. *ˀiiḥ maḥƛii*
ˀi:ḥʷ maḥƛi:
big house
'a big house'

(127) Quantity expression modifying nominal

a. *muu ḥaw̓iɬ*
mu: ḥaw̓iɬ
four chief
'four chiefs'

b. *ˀaƛakʷaɬtaqimɬ ˁuy̓i*
ˀaƛakʷaɬ -taqimɬ ˁuy̓i
eight -bundles medicine
'eight bundles of medicine'

(128) Quantifying expression modifying nominal

a. *ˀaya č̓apac*
ˀaya č̓apac
many canoe
'many canoes'

b. *ˀuuš ˁiniiƛ*
ˀu:š ˁini:ƛ
some dog
'some dogs'

Verbals, on the other hand, are modified by qualifying expressions, but not by those modifying expressions that are associated directly with nominals.

(129) *hiikʷaƚšiˀat* *k̓ʷačšiˀat.*
hi:kʷaƚ -ši(ƛ̓)-ˀa·ƚ *k̓ʷač -ši(ƛ̓)-'at*
nearly -MOM -PL hit.the.right.spot -MOM -SHIFT
they.almost.did hit.the.right.place

'They almost shot him in the right spot.'
'They almost had a direct hit.' [Wolf 132]

(130) *ˀaanisa* *ˁačikšiƛ̓.*
ˀa:ni -sa *ˁačik -ši(ƛ̓)*
really -1sg know.how.to -MOM
I.really learned.how.to

'I really learned how to do it.' [CLLS 121]

The distinction between nominals and verbals is robust in that it represents the point of significant convergence among related but independent semantic and structural patterns. It seems appropriate to consider nominals and verbals to be basic classes in Nuuchahnulth grammar.

3.1.2.2. Adjectivals

In addition to the class distinction between nominals and verbals that divides the whole group of inflectable words, it seems reasonable to recognize another class, ADJECTIVALS. These are a subtype of the verbal class. Adjectivals, however, do not take objects, and they can be combined with a nominal to form a phrase (see section 4.2.2 for the discussion of the domain of PHRASE). Notice that the syntactic relationship between the adjectival and the nominal within the phrase is different from the predicate-argument relationship. In this configuration the adjectival functions as a modifier for the nominal.

(131) *ˀuˀaamits* ***tupkaapiiḥ*** *šuuwis.*
ˀu -'a·p -it -s *tupka:pi:ḥ* *šu:wis*
it -buying-PAST -1sg black shoes

'I bought black shoes.' [elicited CL]

(132) *ˀatquu* ***čamiḥta*** *quuˀas* *qawiqaaƚ.*
ˀat -qu: *čamiḥta* *qu:ˀas*
although-COND.3 proper person NAME

'Although he was a person with proper manners [he was not invited to the feast].'
[Qawiqaalth 12]

Sometimes adjectivals can directly serve as arguments.

(133)	*ˀayaˀiš*		***ƛuł***.
	ˀaya	*-ˀi·š*	*ƛuł*
	many	-IND.3	good
	there.are.many		good.ones

'There are many good ones.' [elicited CL]

Semantically, adjectivals express property concepts and numbers. It might be possible to consider adjectivals to be a semantically defined subgroup within verbals by characterizing their unique behavioral patterns as a function of their semantic properties. However, the potential of combining with a nominal in a syntactic relationship other than as a predicate-argument seems to separate adjectivals significantly enough from other verbals (see Jacobsen 1979a: 136). In addition, the potential to serve directly as an argument, although rather limited, also seems to represent a notable departure from the typical behavior of verbals. Thus, it seems well justified to recognize adjectivals as one of the structurally relevant (rather than purely semantic) word classes.

3.1.2.3. Other Previously Proposed Word Classes

Jacobsen's (1979a) description also includes classes of 'auxiliary verbs', 'prepositions', and 'adverbs' in his inventory of word classes in Nootkan. These classes, however, seem to be based on much less certain grounds. Unlike the class of adjectivals that is based on unique syntactic privileges, these latter three classes cannot be characterized by syntactic behaviors that are decisively different from those of verbals.

3.1.2.3.1. Adverbs?

The class of 'adverbs' is defined by Jacobsen (1979a: 131ff.) as a subclass of intransitive verbals that can be combined with another clause in any order (i.e., the adverb can precede or follow the other clause). Typical 'adverbs' would include *ẏuuqʷaa* 'also', *ˀiiqḥii* 'still', and *ˀaƛčiił* 'for two days'.

(134)	*ẏuuqʷaaˀaṗatƛa*				*tumiis*	*ˀuuḥẇałˀat.*		
	ẏu:qʷa:	*-'ap*	*-'at*	*-ƛa·*	*tumi:s*	*ˀu*	*-ḥẇał*	*-'at*
	also	-CAUS	-SHIFT	-also	charcoal	it	-using	-SHIFT
	also.do				charcoal	used.it		

'[And for the stern part,] charcoal is used there too.' [Canoe 191]

(135) *čamaqƛcuk* *y̓uuqʷaa.*
čamaqƛ -cuk ***y̓u:qʷa:***
take.time -needing also
'You have to be very careful too.' [Canoe 219]

It is, however, difficult to distinguish the structural behavior of such 'adverbs' and that of other intransitive verbals in serialization (see section 4.4.2.1 about serialization):

(136) *waasiḥ* *waaˀat* *kaˀupšiˀat,*
wa:si -ḥ *wa·-'at* *kaˀup -ši(ƛ)-'at*
where -INTER.3 say -SHIFT mention -MOM -SHIFT
where.is.he they.asked mentioned
'"Where is he?", they asked them, mentioning his name.' [Kingfisher 154]

(137) *ˤiḥak* *ɬuucmaˀi* *hiniiˀas.*
ˤiḥ -ak *ɬu:cma -ˀi·* *hin -i:ˀas*
cry -DUR woman -DEF get.there -going.outside
crying the.woman go.out
'The woman was crying as she came out.' [Kingfisher 40]

Jacobsen (1979a: 132) argues that the occurrence of predicative suffixes may well be a superficial phenomenon resulting from the requirement that places these suffixes on the first word of a sentence. Therefore 'adverbs' are not really potentially predicative. He cites as support of his view the fact that the person marking on the sentence-initial 'adverbs' appears to reflect what is appropriate for the following verbal: thus, the 'adverb' takes the person marking not because of its own predicativity but as a result of a mechanical rule that places such marking on the first word. In the following example from Makah (Jacobsen 1979a: 132), the subject and object pronominal suffixes found on the initial 'adverb' are those appropriate for the following predicate. Nuuchahnulth does not have the object pronominal suffix, but the main point of Jacobsen's argument still applies with respect to the subject suffix.

(138) *hu·ˀax̣isi·cux̣* *da·c.*
still-IND.1sg.SUBJ/2.sg.OBJ see
'I can still see you.'

However, it is not clear whether this fact about person marking actually proves a lack or a reduced degree of predicativity of 'adverbs'. It is true that these 'adverbs' do not play any significant role in determining the argument-taking characteristics of the complex predicate, but that seems to be a separate issue, having more to do with their abstract meanings that do not suggest any clear semantic subcategorization frame, rather than with the degree of predicativity. Indeed, words in this 'adverb' class are predicative enough to carry the predicative peripheral suffixes. (Note that nonpredicative words can never carry the predicative suffixes (see the discussion in 2.4.3.2.11.)) Furthermore, they can stand alone structurally as the sole predicate within a clause, as illustrated in the following example:

(139)

y̓uuqʷaa	*čims.*
y̓u:qʷa:	*čims*
also	bear

'Bears are like that too.' [Dog 6]

Thus, the proposal for a class of 'adverbs' does not seem to have a strong justification.

3.1.2.3.2. Prepositions?

A class of 'prepositions' is also difficult to maintain. Jacobsen himself does not present it as a clearly definable class, although he includes it in the list of his proposed word classes. Jacobsen (1979a: 128) points out that many of them are formed on the referential stem *ˀu-*, that they often occur in combination with other predicates (see SERIALIZATION discussed in 4.4.2.1.), and that their meanings are abstract, case-like relationships that are conveyed by English prepositions. However, none of these facts seem to distinguish 'prepositions' clearly from other object-taking verbals. (See section 4.4.2.1 for further discussion and examples.)

To give Jacobsen his due, however, there are indeed a small number of verbals that do function somewhat like English prepositions. The words *ˀuukʷiɬ* and *ˀuuˀatup* below are good examples: they only express abstract relational meanings and normally occur as part of a complex predication.

(140)

naˀaackʷi	*qʷayac̓iik*	***ˀuukʷiɬ***	*quuquuˀas,*
naˀa:-ckʷi·	*qʷayac̓i:k*	*ˀu -kʷiɬ*	DUP *-qu:ˀas*
hear -having.happened	wolf	it -doing.to	DISTR -man
understood	wolf	to.him	people

'Wolves used to understand humans; Wolves used to understand what we say.' [Wolf 38]

(141)

šišaa	***ˀuuˀatup***	*kʷakuucuk,*
šiš -(y)a·	*ˀu -ˀatup*	*kʷaku:c -uk*
clean -CONT	it -doing.for	grandchild -POSS
cleaning	doing.for.them	her.grandchildren

'She would peel them for her g randchildren.' [CLLS 85]

These words with highly specialized functions shed an interesting light on an aspect of structural dynamism in Nuuchahnulth. Functional and distributional specialization can occur as a result of heavy, consistent use in discourse and can result in grammaticization of the function. Thus, the functional and distributional specialization observed with the above words reveals a functional/structural focal point and suggests an aspect of structural dynamism that has a potential for grammaticization. In this sense, we could say that the 'preposition' exists in Nuuchahnulth grammar as a functional/structural focal point and therefore as a *potential* grammatical class. However, it is misleading to equate this structural potential with a true structural category: the structural specialization of 'prepositions' does not reach the level where the class is defined on the basis of a unique set of structural characteristics.

3.1.2.3.3. Auxiliary Verbs?

'Auxiliary verbs' are defined by Jacobsen as 'a kind of intransitive verb limited to occurrence before an absolutive verb form [= verb form without predicative peripheral suffixes]' (1979a: 139f.). The prototypical examples of 'auxiliary verbs' include *wik* 'not', *ˁac̓ik* 'be expert at', *hawiiƛ* 'finish', *č̓in̓uqƛ* 'be unwilling', and *hiikʷaɬ* 'almost'. The following are some example sentences from my data:

(142)	*wik̓ii*	*ˀaaˀaaˀiša.*
	***wik**-'i·*	*ˀa:ˀa:ˀiša·*
	not -IMP.2s	hurry
	don't	hurry

'Don't rush.' [Canoe 199]

(143)	*hiikʷaɬšiƛniš*			*qʷaa*	*ḥaˀii.*	
	hi:kʷaɬ	*-ši(ƛ)*	*-ni·š*	*qʷa:*	*ḥa*	*-ˀi:*
	nearly	-MOM	-IND.1pl	thus	completely-reaching	
	we.almost			thus	go.all.the.way	

'We almost did so [travel] all the way. [We almost got to our destination.]' [CLLS 233]

(144)	*ˁac̓ikšiƛ*		*ḥaaw̓iɬaƛˀi*	*č̓aˀuy̓ic*
	ˁac̓ik	*-ši(ƛ)*	*ḥa:w̓iɬaƛ-ˀi·*	*č̓aˀuš-'i·c*
	know.how.to	-MOM	young.man-DEF	raw -eating
	learned.how.to		the.young.man	eat.raw.food

'The young man learned to eat raw meat.' [Wolf 69]

The need for a class of 'auxiliary verbs' does not seem compelling. It is not clear what is gained from establishing such a class aside from simply the grouping together of intransitive verbals that take a complement clause. Jacobsen's motivation for proposing the class of 'auxiliary verbs' appears to be to capture the syntactic relationship of complementation (see section 4.4.2.3) as a structurally primary relationship that is separate from and independent of the predicate-argument relationship. Although it is important to recognize the complementation relationship in the Nuuchahnulth grammar, it seems problematic to anchor or attribute complementation to a word class of 'auxiliary verbs'. First, 'auxiliary verb' as defined by Jacobsen does not represent an exclusive class of words that take a complement. Some transitive verbals can take either a complement clause or a nominal object. For example, *naˀa:* 'hear' takes a complement clause in (145) and a nominal object in (146).

(145)	*naˀaaˀaƛ̓*	***qii***	***wiinapi***	***qʷayač̓iikˀi.***	
	naˀa:-'aƛ̓	*qi:*	*wi:napi*	*qʷayač̓i:k-*	*ˀi·*
	hear -TEL	for.a.long.time	remaining	wolf	-DEF
	they.heard	for.a.long.time	remaining	the.wolves	

'They heard the wolves remaining there for a long time.' [Wolf 63]

(146)	*naˀaaˀat*	***maan̓uuˀisˀatḥiicˀi***		***č̓iiqy̓ak.***
	naˀa:-'at	*ma:n̓u:ˀisˀatḥ-i:c*	*-ˀi·*	*č̓i:q-y̓ak*
	hear -SHIFT	Manhousat -belonging.to	-DEF	sing -instrument.for
	it.was.heard	thing.belonging.to.Manhousats		song

'They heard the Manhousat songs.' [Wolf 57]

Thus, 'auxiliary verbs' cannot be uniquely characterized as a class of complement-taking verbals.

Second, the fact that there are transitive verbals that can take either a nominal object or a complement clause may suggest that the complementation relationship is not fundamentally different from the predicate-argument relationship. If this is the case, 'auxiliary verbs' can be considered just a subtype of transitive verbals that only take complements.

Given the uncertainty concerning the motivation and justification for this class, it seems prudent at this time not to recognize 'auxiliary verbs' as a separate word class in Nuuchahnulth.

3.1.2.4. Summary of the Proposed Word Classes

NOMINALS

i) Unmarked function
The default function of a nominal is referring (see Hopper and Thompson 1984).
- When a nominal is presented in isolation, it is most likely to be interpreted as an expression referring to an object or a referable concept.
- Nominals can serve as predicates, but only in a limited way — only as existential, classifying, or identifying expressions.

ii) Modification
Nominals can be modified by quantifying expressions, quantity expressions, and property concepts.

iii) Semantics
Typically nominals designate entities.

VERBALS

i) Unmarked function
The default function of a verbal is predicating.
- Verbals cannot serve directly as arguments (except when 'implicit derivation' can be applied): they must be nominalized first.

ii) Modification
Verbals can be modified by qualifying expressions.

iii) Semantics
Verbals typically express dynamic concepts, relational concepts, and attributive concepts.

ADJECTIVALS

— Adjectivals constitute a subtype of one-place ('intransitive') verbals.

i) Combinatory possibility
Adjectivals can combine as a modifier with a nominal to form a phrase.

ii) Syntactic function
Sometimes adjectivals can serve directly as arguments.

3.1.2.5. The Nature of Word Classes in Nuuchahnulth

The proposed word classes are real in the morphosyntactic structure of Nuuchahnulth in that they represent converging points of various functional and structural patterns occurring in the language. In other words, word classes are indeed meaningful and useful in capturing the structural patterns in Nuuchahnulth. However, it is important to keep in mind that Nuuchahnulth word classes are very different in nature from similarly named lexical categories in English. In traditional descriptions, of English lexical categories appear to be very elaborate (= consisting of many categories), highly specialized (= consisting of narrowly and clearly bounded categories), and highly grammaticized (i.e., very deeply entrenched in formal arrangements of grammar). In Nuuchahnulth the structural differentiation among words is not nearly as elaborate, absolute, or grammaticized as English. Word-class distinctions in Nuuchahnulth are much less specialized functionally and structurally and are small in number. The boundaries between the classes are fuzzy. And more important, the word classes are not so grammaticized, in that they are defined largely on the basis of functional and behavioral propensities within morphosyntactic structuring rather than direct and fixed association with certain forms such as inflections or grammatical categories. In other words, word classes in Nuuchahnulth are not as directly and rigidly anchored to forms or grammatical categories.

The low degree of specialization and grammaticization of the word classes can also be seen in the fact that the syntactic relationship among words is often ambiguous in Nuuchahnulth. In languages with highly grammaticized lexical categories, such as English, the categoriality can be rigid enough to project a relatively clear syntactic structure. In Nuuchahnulth, however, words do not suggest as much about the syntactic structure surrounding them. For example, in the sequence of words *many cod* in English it is clear that *many* is modifying a noun *cod.* In contrast, in the Nuuchahnulth equivalent *ˀaya tuškuuḥ* the relationship between the two words is ambiguous: *ˀaya* can be expressing a predicate and *tuškuuḥ* expressing an argument, which could be translated as 'cod were many'; or *ˀaya* can be modifying the meaning of *tuškuuḥ*, which could be translated as 'there are many cod' or simply 'many cod'.

In sum, word classes in Nuuchahnulth are not so much structural categories as behavioral categories: they represent groups of words defined by a set of regularities that are formed and maintained through repeated use in discourse rather than purely structural properties. Because they are not grammatically very rigid, these word classes may be felt to be 'loose' and semantically and functionally motivated to a greater degree than lexical categories in English.

3.2. Internal Structure of the Word

Languages differ significantly in what can be expressed in a word. One of the most important typological factors in this respect is the degree of morphological synthesis allowed in a language. Nuuchahnulth represents a group of languages that are on the most complex end of the spectrum in terms of possible morphological synthesis — languages that are often characterized as 'polysynthetic'. As illustrated in the examples below, a word can have a highly complex internal structure in Nuuchahnulth, thanks to numerous lexical suffixes. (Lexical suffixes are indicated in bold.)

(147) *hiyisimyiɬʔaƛqʷin*
hiɬ ***-ʻis*** ***-imɬ*** ***-'iɬ*** *-'aƛ -qʷin*
be.there -being.on.the.beach -being.in.a.group -being.in.the.house-TEL -COND.1pl
'We used to get together in a house on the beach.' [CLLS 171]

(148) *čiḥwaḥsuɬmaḥsap*
čiḥ ***-waḥsuɬ*** ***-maḥsa*** *-'ap*
spirit -going.out -wanting.to -CAUS
'He wants a spirit to leave.' [Canoe 11]

In this section I discuss how a root and lexical suffixes can interact to shape the meaning, and thus the basic syntactic characteristics, of a word in Nuuchahnulth.

3.2.1. Characteristics of Roots and Lexical Suffixes

3.2.1.1. Roots

A root is a morphological base of a word in that every word is required to contain one, but it is not necessarily independent in terms of distribution.

Crosslinguistically, roots commonly play a central role in determining the semantic and syntactic characteristics of a word. In many cases this is also true in Nuuchahnulth, but it is hardly a norm. As we will see below in the discussion of lexical suffixes, a root can play a peripheral role in relation to a lexical suffix in determining the overall semantic and syntactic characteristics of a word.

In terms of the semantic characteristics of the inventory of roots, those expressing entities, events, and states seem to constitute the majority. A very small number of roots express quality, quantity, time, location, and demonstrative notions.

3.2.1.2. Lexical Suffixes

Lexical suffixes are morphologically dependent and must be associated with a root. Lexical suffixes in Nuuchahnulth are typologically unusual as suffixes in that they are numerous (there are more than 400) and have concrete lexical meanings. In terms of meaning, lexical suffixes expressing locations, events, and states are all roughly equally numerous. Those expressing entities are not as numerous as others, but the group is by no means small. Although there is a significant overlap between the types of meanings expressed by roots and those expressed by lexical suffixes, there are a few notable differences between them. First, locative notions are almost exclusively expressed by lexical suffixes. When locations need to be referred to as such, a word is formed by attaching a locative lexical suffix to a semantically rather empty stem.

(149)
    a. *hiẏaqƛ* 'inside'
        < *hił* 'be there' + *-'aqƛ* 'being inside'
    b. *hiłsłuuqs* '(at) the corner inside a canoe'
        < *hił* 'be there' + *-słu:qs* 'being at the corner inside a canoe'
    c. *hiiłčaaqił* '(at) the rear end of the house'
        < *hił* 'be there' + *-ča·qił* 'being at the rear end of the house'
    d. *ʔapquuʔa* '(at) the rocky point'
        < *ʔap-* LOCATIVE ROOT + *-qu:* 'being at a point' + *-'a·* 'being on the rock'

The second respect in which lexical suffixes and roots differ has to do with groups of morphemes that express entities. The proportion of morphemes that express entities is smaller in the inventory of lexical suffixes than in that of roots. In other words, in relative terms, lexical suffixes expressing entities are fewer than roots expressing entities. Furthermore, entities expressed by lexical suffixes are abstract, general classes of things, whereas those expressed by roots are more specific. Following are lists of selected lexical suffixes and roots that express entities.

(150) Lexical suffixes expressing entities
    a. **-uł** 'place for'
       hałinquł 'bathing place' < *hałinq-* 'bathing' + **-uł**
       naquwił 'pub' < *naq-* 'drink' + **-uł** + *-'ił* 'being in the house'
       saantiquwił 'church house' < *sa:ntiq-* 'Sunday' + **-uł** + *-'ił* 'being in the house'

b. ***-y̓akʷ ~ -č̓akʷ*** 'instrument for'
haw̓ač̓ak 'utensils; wooden cooking pot' < *haw̓a-* 'food' + ***-č̓akʷ***
ˤasy̓ak 'carving tools' < *ˤas-* 'carve; do carpenter work' + ***-y̓akʷ***
ʔiiqḥy̓ak 'mythology, teachings' < *ʔiiqḥ-* 'narrate' + ***-y̓akʷ***

c. ***-tu·p*** 'thing, species'
naqtuup 'beverage' < *naq-* 'drink' + ***-tu·p***
m̓uč̓ičtup 'clothes' < *m̓uč̓ič-* 'clothed' + ***-tu·p***
haptuup 'fur-bearing animal' < *hap-* 'fur' + ***-tu·p***
quʔactup 'mankind, human beings' < *quʔac-* 'human' + ***-tu·p***

(151) Roots expressing entities
ˤuy̓i 'medicine'
muwač 'deer'
kuukuḥw̓isa 'hair seal'
maḥt̓ii 'house'

This difference in the nature of the entities expressed is interesting in light of the general pattern found in the alternation between the morphological and syntactic expressions of a participant. As I discuss in more detail in a later section (4.6.1), when a participant in an event can be expressed either morphologically within a word or syntactically as an argument, the choice of encoding strategy strongly correlates with referentiality. Thus, a generic, nonparticular participant tends to be expressed morphologically, while a particular, individuated participant tends to be expressed syntactically. Considering that lexical suffixes are always part of a morphological complex and can never be syntactically independent words, it seems appropriate for lexical suffixes to express only abstract, general classes of entities.

In terms of the functional role played in word-building, lexical suffixes can affect the semantic, and consequently the syntactic, characteristics of a word in highly idiosyncratic and dramatic ways. For example, in (152), the verbal root *hatk-* 'roll' does not take any object. But with the addition of the lexical suffix *-miʔa* 'moving on (the rock)', the resulting predicate can take a direct argument expressing a location (*m̓uukuukʔi* 'the rocks' below) in addition to the agentive argument.

(152) *haatkhaatkmiʔa* ***m̓uukuukʔi***.
REDUP:- *hatk* ***-miʔa*** *m̓u:ku:k -ʔi·*
ITER- roll -moving.on.(the.rock) rock -DEF
roll.repeatedly.on the.rocks
'They roll and roll on the rocks.' [Gray Whale 13]

Similarly, in (153), the root *ƛaps-* 'dive' only takes an agent, but with the suffix *-ʔatu* 'sinking into (the water)' the complex predicate can take an agent and an object identifying a location. Here the location *c̓aʔak* 'river' serves as the object.

(153) ***c̓aʔak*** *ƛaapsʔataƛquuč.*
c̓aʔak ƛaps ***-ʔatu*** *-'aƛ -qu: -č*
river dive -sinking.into.(the.water) -TEL -COND.3 -INF
river would.dive.into
'He would dive into the river every once in a while.' [Mink 220]

Lexical suffixes do not uniformly affect the semantic and syntactic characteristics of a resulting complex word. The lexical suffixes have traditionally been divided into 'governing' and 'restrictive' types (Sapir and Swadesh 1939; Swadesh 1939; Rose 1981). 'Governing' lexical suffixes 'introduce a new central notion to which the underlying stem or theme becomes subsidiary' (Sapir and Swadesh 1939: 236). In other words, the 'governing' lexical suffixes assume a central role in determining the general semantic characteristics of the resulting stem. In the following examples, the lexical suffixes *-'i·c* 'consuming' and *-yi:q* 'traveling in' seem to be the semantically central elements in each word: they function semantically like predicates that take the nominal root as an argument.

(154) Lexical suffix classified as 'governing' type

a. *ʕuy̓iic*
ʕuy̓i ***-'i·c***
medicine -consuming
'take medicine' [CLLS 323]

b. *č̓apyiiʕaƛ*
č̓ap ***-yi:q*** *-'aƛ*
canoe -traveling.in-TEL
'He traveled in a canoe.' [Wolf 35]

'Restrictive' lexical suffixes, on the other hand, add a notion that modifies or amplifies the underlying theme rather than introducing a new core theme to the morphological complex. Thus, in (155a), it is the root *č̓i:q-* 'attack' that shapes the overall meaning of the word, while the lexical suffix *-'aqa* 'severally doing ...' simply modifies the meaning of the root. Similarly, in (155b) the root *su-* 'hold' seems to play the central role in shaping the meaning of the complex word, with the lexical suffix *-'iɬ* 'being in the house' modifying the meaning of the root.

(155) Lexical suffix classified as 'restrictive' type

a. *či'ʕaqaƛquuč'ʔaɬ,*
či:q ***-'aqa*** *-'aƛ -qu: -č -ʔa·ɬ*
fight -severally.doing -TEL -COND.3 -INF -PL
'They would fight.' [Qawiqaalth 119]

b. *suʔiɬʔaƛquu*
su ***-'iɬ*** *-'aƛ -qu:*
hold -being.in.the.house -TEL -COND.3
'She used to keep her in the house.' [CLLS 80]

The distinction between 'governing' and 'restrictive' types is convenient in speaking of relationships between a root and a lexical suffix in the most general terms. However, the traditional characterization of the distinction in terms of subclasses among lexical suffixes is rather misleading, since the distinction has been defined on the basis of semantic observations rather than formal characteristics: that is, there is no formal difference associated uniquely with 'governing' and 'restrictive' types. In this sense, the distinction is not really a property of lexical suffixes themselves, but of the meanings expressed by lexical suffixes.

Defining a linguistic category solely on the basis of semantic observations often leaves a question of whether the definition is just an interpretive artifact, and unfortunately the distinction between 'governing' and 'restrictive' is not an exception. In fact, Boas (1947: 237) rejects the distinction introduced by Sapir and Swadesh by arguing that it is not 'based on internal evidence, but rather on our European classifications':

> For instance [the morphological complex] "to see a canoe" which [includes a lexical suffix expressing the notion of "to see" that] would fall under the heading of "governing suffixes" may as well be conceived as "to perform an action relating to a canoe by seeing" in which case [the lexical suffix expressing] "to see" would be a restrictive element. ... It is impossible to decide how these combinations may be felt by native speakers. (Ibid.)

Boas's point is well taken, given that the distinction was defined on the basis of an abstract semantic configuration. However, complete rejection of the distinction between 'governing' and 'restrictive' types does not lead to a rich and insightful description of the use of lexical suffixes either. For example, compare (156) and (157) below. They have similar internal structures, with a nominal root followed by a lexical suffix. The only significant difference between the two is that the lexical suffix in (156) *-i:ɬ* 'making' would belong to the 'governing' type, and the suffix in (157) *-'aqƛ* 'being inside' to the 'restrictive' type. If there is no difference between the 'governing' and 'restrictive' types, we would expect them to be indistinguishable.

(156) *čaapaciiłẇiłas*
čapac **-i:ł** -*ẇiłas*
canoe -making -about.to
'He is going to make a canoe.' [Canoe 1]

(157) *quʔačaqƛ*
quʔac **-'aqƛ**
person -being.inside
'There is a person inside.' [Canoe 9]

But when we examine the discourse structure following the above examples, a very interesting pattern emerges. The entity expressed by the nominal root in (156), i.e., *canoe*, is not tracked in the following discourse at all. The speaker proceeds to talk about how to select a tree suitable for a canoe. In contrast, the entity expressed in (157) *person* is tracked and elaborated in the following discourse. This difference in discourse tracking can be viewed as a difference in what aspect of a predication is made salient in the word. Thus, the entity designated by the root is discourse-salient and is meant to be tracked in (157) but not in (156). In rough terms, we could say that the root in (157), but not that in (156), plays a central role in the complex word. Interestingly, this difference in the role played by the root is exactly what is suggested in the classification of the suffix in (157) as 'restrictive' and that in (156) as 'governing'. This pattern is not absolutely regular, but it nonetheless seems to be representative of the majority of cases.

Thus, in discourse terms, the distinction between the 'governing' and 'restrictive' types of lexical suffixation can be given a noninterpretive definition and provides a meaningful account of patterns of use of lexical suffixes. And therefore I believe that the distinction should be maintained in a discussion of the use of lexical suffixes. At the same time, the distinction between 'governing' and 'restrictive' that seems useful is different in nature from that proposed by Sapir and Swadesh. The distinction is based on observable effects on discourse structure, and therefore it is relevant only when such effects are discernible. At this point, the distinction has been found relevant only in the above illustrated structural context: i.e., when lexical suffixes are associated with a nominal root. Note that this is in sharp contrast with the traditional formulation of the distinction, where the distinction between 'governing' and 'restrictive' is universally applicable, dividing the inventory of lexical suffixes into two classes.

Also note that, just as in its traditional formulation, the discourse-based distinction between 'governing' and 'restrictive' is not strictly a property of lexical suffixes but is a property of what is expressed by the lexical suffixes. Nonetheless, the distinction is descriptively useful in clarifying different ways in which lexical suffixes can participate in the formation of semantic and syntactic characteristics of a complex word.

3.2.2. Types of Relationships between Stems and Lexical Suffixes

This section lays out different types of semantic relationships that a lexical suffix can have with a stem.

3.2.2.1. Object + Predicate

Some lexical suffixes can serve as predicates that take the entity expressed by the stem as a notional object (including patient, theme, location).

(158) *ʕu̓y̓iic̓ap̓at,*
ʕuy̓i ***-'i·c*** *-'ap* *-'at*
medicine -consuming -CAUS -SHIFT
STEM LEX.SUFF
'making me take medicine' [CLLS 328]

(159) *č̓aapaciiłʔaƛquu,*
č̓apac -i:ł *-'aƛ -qu:*
canoe -making -TEL -COND.3
STEM LEX.SUFF
'when making a canoe' [Canoe 143]

(160) *ƚ̓aatn̓anak̓aƛ̓atquu*
ƚ̓a:tn̓a -na·k *-'aƛ -'at -qu:*
children -having -TEL -SHIFT -COND.3
STEM LEX.SUFF
'when you have children' [CLLS 128]

3.2.2.2. Complement + Higher Predicate

Some lexical suffixes can serve as higher predicates that take the verbal notion expressed by the stem as a complement.

(161) *kuučiy̓as.*
ku:čił -'as
fillet.fish -going.in.order.to
STEM LEX.SUFF
'travel to make dried fish' [CLLS 28]

(162) *wik haaɬaaˀiiḥ, wiik̓iiḥ.*
wik ***haɬa·*** ***-'i:ḥ*** *wik-'i:ḥ*
not pay -trying.to.get not -trying.to.get
STEM LEX.SUFF
'not trying to get paid' [CLLS 102]

Example (163) involves two complement-taking lexical suffixes, *-'i:ḥ* 'trying to get' and *-maḥsa* 'wanting to'.

(163) *huuḥtakšiiḥmaḥsa*
huḥtak*-ši(ƛ)-****'i:ḥ*** ***-maḥsa***
know -MOM -trying.to.get -wanting.to
STEM LEX.SUFF LEX.SUFF
'want to learn how to' [GLLS 174]

3.2.2.3. Modifier + Nominal

Some lexical suffixes express generic entities. When associated with this type of lexical suffix, the stem serves to provide additional specific information about the entity designated by the lexical suffix, functioning semantically like a modifier of the lexical suffix.

(164) ***-maˤuk*** 'one skilled in ...'

a. *č̓aapaciiɬmaˤuk*
č̓apac -i:ɬ ***-maˤuk***
canoe -making -one.skilled.in
'one who is skilled in making a canoe' [Canoe 9]

b. *suusmaˤuk*
sus ***-maˤuk***
swim-one.skilled.in
'one who is skilled in swimming' [elicited 7.29.91-84]

c. *huuɬmaˤuk*
hu:ɬ ***-maˤuk***
dance -one.skilled.in
'one who is skilled in dancing' [elicited 7.31.91-3]

d. *kaamatqmaˤuk*
kamatq ***-maˤuk***
run -one.skilled.in
'one who is skilled in running' [elicited 7.29.91-13]

(165) ***-y̓akʷ*** 'instrument for ...'
a. *kimty̓ak*
kimt ***-y̓akʷ***
pry -instrument.for
'lever' [Canoe 50]

b. *č̓aḥy̓ak,*
č̓aḥ ***-y̓akʷ***
adze -instrument.for
'adze' [Canoe 79]

c. *c̓uuƛ̓c̓uuyay̓ak,*
REDUP- *c̓u* *-(y)a* ***-y̓akʷ***
ITER- wash -REP - instrument.for
'basin' [CLLS 83]

d. *ḥaaḥuupay̓ak.*
ḥa:ḥu:p *-(y)a·*-***y̓akʷ***
teaching -CONT - instrument.for
'teachings' [CLLS 259]

3.2.2.4. Numeral + Classifier

Some lexical suffixes are attached to numeral roots and express a unit of measurement or serve as a classifier.

(166) *ḥayučił*
ḥayu ***-či·ł***
ten -days.long
'for ten days' [GLLS 50]

(167) *muuy̓ał*
mu: ***-y̓ał***
four -fathoms
'four fathoms' [Canoe 22]

(168) *ˀaƛista*
*ˀaƛa-**ista***
two -passengers.on.board
'two passengers on board' [Kingfisher 9]

3.2.2.5. Predicate + Adverbial

Some lexical suffixes express various adverbial notions, including location and manner, associated with stems expressing actions, events, or states. Examples (169)–(171) illustrate lexical suffixes with locative notions and (172)–(173) show those expressing manner-like notions.

(169) *ƚaapsˀatu*
*ƚaps **-ˀatu***
dive -sinking.into.water
'dive into the water' [Mink 39]

(170) *ẇašˁaqƛ̓asna,*
*ẇašq **-'aqƛ̓as** -na·*
bunched.together -being.in.the.house-1pl
'It was crowded in our house.' [CLLS 6]

(171) *k̓ʷak̓ʷayimƛ*
*k̓ʷa **-yimƛ***
get.broken -being.on.the.shoulder
'broke the shoulder' [CLLS 302]

(172) *hupiisƚaƚˀaƛquuˀaƚ*
*hupi· **-sƚaƚ** -'aƛ -qu: -ˀa·ƚ*
help -doing.reciprocally -TEL -COND.3`-PL
'They helped each other.' [CLLS 67]

(173) *naˀaataḥ.*
*naˀa: **-ataḥ***
hear -trying.to.catch
'She listened carefully.' [Qawiqaalth 29]

3.2.3. On the Nature of Morphological Complexity

A discussion of the nature of morphological complexity is in order. Although morphological analyzability may suggest that internally complex words are formed through a fully productive compositional process, that conclusion is simplistic and idealized. Speakers indeed seem to have some awareness of the internal structure of the word (or more accurately, patterns that suggests the internal structure), although the degree of awareness varies greatly depending on the lexical suffixes in the word. This awareness is evidenced in the following creative form produced by a young speaker:

(174) *muwač̓ic* 'eating deer' < *muwač* 'deer' [independent form] + -*'i·c* 'consuming'
conservative form: *muw̓iic* < *muw-* 'deer' [root form] + -*'i·c* 'consuming'

The creative form *muwač̓ic* could not have been produced if the speaker were not aware of the pattern based on the lexical suffix -*'i·c* 'consuming'. Nuuchahnulth then seems to allow productive and compositional predicate formation more than other languages, such as English, do. However, cases like the lexical suffix -*'i·c* 'consuming' are too limited to be considered the norm. Many combinations of multiple lexical morphemes are treated as unanalyzable chunks. As pointed out by various researchers (e.g., Mithun 1984), different aspects of compositional processes in a language are subject to 'lexicalization', where a certain combination of constituting elements becomes registered through repeated uses in a lexical depository as a single meaningful element. Speakers treat such a lexicalized combination of elements as a set and produce it by retrieving the set rather than by combining the constituting elements every time. Undoubtedly Nuuchahnulth is no exception in this regard. Lexical derivation in Nuuchahnulth is susceptible to lexicalization, and therefore we must be careful not to assume that all morphologically complex predicates are in fact built on-the-fly.

Thus, compositionality characterizes the structural potential rather than the foundation of all instances of word formation in Nuuchahnulth. The structural resource of lexical suffixes allows some degree of compositional formation of a word if it is necessary, but this composition is neither a norm nor a necessary process.

4

THE STRUCTURAL ORGANIZATION OF NUUCHAHNULTH SYNTAX

In this chapter I discuss the nature of syntactic structure and patterns found in the syntactic organization of words in Nuuchahnulth. In section 4.1 I distinguish different types of relationships identified in the syntactic patternings in Nuuchahnulth. Section 4.2 lays out different structural domains that are relevant to syntactic structuring in the language. In 4.3 I discuss the nature of the argument structure in Nuuchahnulth. Thus, the first three sections of this chapter provide characterizations of syntactic structuring in Nuuchahnulth at the most basic levels. The sections that follow provide descriptions of different structural strategies of building complex syntactic constructions and of various structural alternations in the domain of syntax. Section 4.4 lays out syntactic strategies for building nominal and verbal complexes. Section 4.5 deals with different ways of manipulating the configuration of participants. In 4.6 I discuss how speakers choose an encoding strategy when there is more than one way of encoding similar semantic content. And finally, in 4.7 I discuss patterns found in the relative ordering of arguments.

4.1. Relationships between Words

Nuuchahnulth has few grammatical markers or formal indicators of different syntactic relationships; therefore there is little formal basis for positing many distinct syntactic relationships among words. Lack of grammaticized lexical categories also makes it difficult to distinguish syntactic relations on the basis of inherent characteristics of combined words. This difficulty prompted Swadesh (1939: 78) to describe syntactic relations in Nuuchahnulth as follows:

> Supplementation is the only type of relation ever involved in external syntax. The supplementation may be to the expressed subject of the predicative word, to the implied object, or to any other of the elements of meaning contained or implied in a word. Interrelationships are not indicated exactly; even word order is loose and is therefore not an unequivocal means of indicating what is supplemental to what.

This statement, as Jacobsen (1979a) argues, is an oversimplification to the extent that it suggests that words are related in the same way regardless of their functions or meanings. The nature of relationships among words can be very different across different structural environments. Moreover, it is possible to identify a limited number of general types among different kinds of syntactic relationship. Thus, if we do not recognize the differences, our description of syntactic structuring patterns in Nuuchahnulth will be impoverished.

At this point, I find it reasonable to recognize four types of syntactic relationships: ARGUMENTHOOD, MODIFICATION, SERIALIZATION, and COMPLEMENTATION. These different syntactic relationships are not something that Nuuchahnulth grammar 'codes' directly. They emerge as a function of the semantics of expressions and their structural domain. Whenever one names distinctions, there is the danger of believing that the named distinctions or classes have an a priori status in the grammar. Swadesh's caution against suggesting a priori syntactic relationships cannot be emphasized enough.

4.1.1. Argumenthood

In Nuuchahnulth one can distinguish words that express predicative notions (e.g., action, event, state, and relation) from those that express entities associated with predicative notions. When they are associated with each other in a syntactically direct relationship in the sense that there is no syntactic mediation between the two (i.e., there is no word serving to relate the two), the predicative word and the words expressing entities are in the PREDICATE–ARGUMENT relationship. For example, in (175) *hiistmaƛits* 'I was born there' is a predicate and *maaqtusiis* 'Maaqtusiis (place name)' is an argument. Similarly in (176), *kʷiisḥiip̓aƛ* 'taste differently, strangely' is a predicate and *c̓aʔak* 'water' is an argument.

(175) *maaqtusiis hiistmaƛits.*
ma:qtusi:s hist -maƛ -it -s
NAME get.there -being.born -PAST -1sg
NAME I.was.born.there
ARGUMENT PREDICATE
'I was born in Maaqtusiis.' [CLLS 2]

(176) *kʷiisḥiip̓aƛ c̓aʔak.*
kʷis -ḥi· -p̓aƛ c̓aʔak
different -DUR -having.taste.of water
taste.differently water
PREDICATE ARGUMENT
'The water tasted strange.' [Kingfisher 25]

A word on the predicate is in order. As we will see below, in Nuuchahnulth a unitary predication denoting a single event can be expressed with a combination of multiple predicates.

4.1.2. Modification

MODIFICATION is a syntactic relationship between words where the function of one word is limited to restricting the interpretation of the head word. For a detailed discussion, see sections 4.4.1.2 and 4.4.2.2. In the following examples, *ˀaya* 'many', *ˀiiḥit* 'was greatly', and *ƛuɬaqak* 'very' are in a modification relationship to *tukuuk* 'sea lion' and *ƛuɬ* 'good', respectively.

(177)

ˀaya	*tukuuk.*
ˀaya	*tuku:k*
many	sea.lion

'There were many kinds of sea lion.' [Qawiqaalth 197]

(178)

ˀiiḥit		*ƛuɬ.*
ˀi:ḥʷ	*-it*	*ƛuɬ*
greatly	-PAST	good

'It was very nice.' [CLLS 8]

(179)

ˀuchinƛ			***ƛuɬaqakˀi***				*ḥaakʷaaƛ,*
ˀu	*-cḥi*	*-in(ƛ)*	*ƛuɬ-aq*		*-ak*	*-ˀi·*	*ḥa:kʷa:ƛ*
it	-being.married.to	-MOM	nice	-very	-DUR	-DEF	girl
get.married.to.her			very.beautiful				girl

'He got married to the very beautiful girl.' [Mink 287]

4.1.3. Serialization

SERIALIZATION is a syntactic relationship between two predicates that are combined to express a unitary state of affairs. A detailed discussion of SERIALIZATION is found in section 4.4.2.1. In the following examples, two predicates are combined to express a unitary event.

(180) *huuˀakˀaƛquus* *mamuuk.*
hu:ˀak-'aƛ -qu:s *mamu:k*
early -TEL -COND.1sg work
I.would.do.early work
PREDICATE 1 **PREDICATE 2**
'I would work early.' [GLLS 147]

(181) *Royal Museum* *ˀucḥinˀaƛs* *mamuuk*
ˀu -cḥin -'aƛ -s *mamu:k*
it -doing.for-TEL -1sg work
I.did.for.it work
PREDICATE 1 **PREDICATE 2**
'I worked for the Royal Museum.' [GLLS 157]

4.1.4. Complementation

COMPLEMENTATION is a syntactic relationship that a clause or a predication can have with a main predicate, where the clause or predication semantically supplements the notion expressed by the main predicate (see sections 4.2.1 and 4.2.3 for the terms CLAUSE and PREDICATION, respectively). For a detailed discussion of COMPLEMENTATION, see section 4.4.2.3. In the following examples, *haptšiƛ* 'hide' and *ˀuyiiˀat haˀumštup* 'give them food' are in a complementation relationship to *ˤaċik* 'be expert at' and *numaak* 'be forbidden', respectively.

(182) *ˤaċik* ***haptšiƛ,***
ˤaċik *hapt-ši(ƛ)*
be.expert.at hide -MOM
'He is good at hiding.' [Mink 17]

(183) *numaak* ***ˀuyiiˀat*** ***haˀumštup***
numa:k *ˀu -ayi· -'at* *haˀum-štu·p*
be.forbidden it -giving -SHIFT food -thing
'It is forbidden to give them food.' [Dog 9]

4.2. Domains of Syntactic Patterning

The domains discussed in this section are those that are justified and motivated within the syntactic patterns found in discourse, and therefore their shape has much to do with the discourse-pragmatic dynamism that governs syntactic patterning. These domains are structurally relevant in that patterns in the syntax can be accounted for with reference to them. However, these domains are not necessarily grammaticized in Nuuchahnulth: there is no grammatical marker or mechanism that directly encodes or is inherently associated with these domains. Consequently, it is not productive to define these domains purely on the basis of form.

4.2.1. The Clause

A combination of a predicate and its arguments forms a syntactic domain, a CLAUSE. A CLAUSE can serve by itself as the core of a predication or can combine with another clause to form a complex predication. (See section 4.2.3 for a detailed discussion of PREDICATION.) Example (184) is a single clause serving as a core of the predication, while example (185) illustrates multiple clauses combining to form a complex predication.

(184)	*ˀunaak*	*k̓ʷak̓ʷaƛ.*
	ˀu -na·k	*k̓ʷak̓ʷaƛ*
	it -having	sea.otter
	have.it	sea.otter

'They had sea otter hide.' [Kingfisher 32]

(185)	*łaapsˀatu*	*qawiqaał,*	*tukuuk*	*ˀukʷink.*
	łaps -ˀatu	*qawiqa:ł*	*tuku:k*	*ˀu -kʷink*
	dive -sinking.into.water	Qawiqaalth	sea.lion	it -being.together.with
	dive.into.water	Qawiqaalth	sea.lion	be.together.with.it
	← CLAUSE 1 →		← CLAUSE 2 →	

'Qawiqaalth dove into the sea with the sea lion.' [Qawiqaalth 171]

Identification of the domain of the clause is motivated by the fact that the clause configuration, i.e., the combination of a predicate and its arguments, does not arise from the lexicon. In Nuuchahnulth the distinction between PREDICATE and ARGUMENT cannot be described in terms of lexical categories that are defined semantically or otherwise. Inflectable words in Nuuchahnulth, which constitute a major portion of the lexicon, are all potentially predicative; they can serve as predicates without overt derivation, and they cannot be classified into grammaticized lexical classes such as nouns or verbs.[1] This makes it impossible in Nuuchahnulth to identify ARGUMENTS and PREDICATES on the basis of the inherent lexical category of words, e.g., [verb = PREDICATE] or [noun = ARGUMENT]. Thus, the distinction between PREDICATE and ARGUMENT cannot be explained as a bottom-up projection from the lexical categories. Instead, the distinction

---

[1] See section 3.1 for a detailed discussion of word classes in Nuuchahnulth.

must be assumed to emerge in the very process of combining multiple words into a discourse functional unit. In other words, the distinction between PREDICATE and ARGUMENT is imposed on words by the higher structure. This top-down imposition suggests the presence of a CLAUSE as a structural domain.

The domain of CLAUSE is comparable in Nuuchahnulth and English in that it consists of a single predicative word and its arguments. However, the 'clauses' in these two languages are different in nature and occur in very different structural environments. They play different roles in syntactic and discourse structuring.

The clause in English represents a domain of a higher structural order in the sense that it can have a high degree of internal complexity with a number of hierarchically arranged subcomponents (i.e., phrases) serving highly specialized structural functions. The English clause also represents a fairly rigid domain of structuring — rigid enough to motivate a high degree of functional specialization and grammaticization as evidenced in its robust lexical and syntactic categories.

In Nuuchahnulth, however, such internal complexity cannot be found within the domain that centers on the combination of a predicate and its argument. In English much of the internal complexity within the clause is introduced by adverbs (or adverbial phrases) and prepositional phrases. Information introduced by such elements in English must be expressed in Nuuchahnulth by a combination of multiple clauses. Sentences (186) and (187) below contain temporal elements that could be expressed with adverbs or a prepositional phrase in English. In Nuuchahnulth the same information needs to be introduced with separate clauses as in *huu̧ʔakitwaʔišʔaał* '(they) used to do it early' in (186) and *ʔaatḥšiƛ* 'as it became night' in (187).

(186)	***huuʔakitwaʔišʔaał***	*ƛimkšiƛ*	*quuʔas*
	hu:ʔak-it -wa·ʔi·š -ʔa:ł	*ƛimk -ši(ƛ)*	*qu:ʔas*
	early -PAST -QUOT.3 -always	awake -MOM	person
	used.to.do.early	wake.up	person

'Long ago, they say, people used to wake up early in the morning.' [Gray Whale 19]

(187)	*čiiqaaʔaƛquuč*	***ʔaatḥšiƛ.***
	či:q-(y)a· -'aƛ -qu: -č	*ʔatḥ -ši(ƛ)*
	sing -CONT -TEL -COND.3 -INF	night -GRAD
	used.to.sing.songs	becoming.night

'He used to sing his song at night.' [Wolf 68]

In sentences (188) and (189) information that could be expressed with a locative prepositional phrase in English is expressed by a clause.

(188)

ʔucačiƛ	*qaay̓uuk̓ʷatḥ*	***hiłstiis***	***takwiiʔa.***
ʔu -ca -či(ƛ)	*qa:y̓u:k̓ʷatḥ*	*hił -sti·s*	*tak -wi:ʔa*
it -going.to -MOM	Kyuquot	be.there -moving.to.the.interior	head.to -being.out.of.the.inlet
went.to.it	Kyuquot	the.head.of.the.bay	going.out.of.the.inlet

'They went to Kyuquot at the head of the bay going out of the inlet.' [Wolf 66]

(189)

yacaaqtuu	***ʔucačiƛ***	***ʔuuƛaqči.***
yac -a·qtu·	*ʔu -ca -či(ƛ)*	*ʔu:ƛaqči*
step -going.over	it -going.to -MOM	Odlaqutla
walked.over	went.there	Odlaqutla

'They went over [the high land] to Odlaqutla.' [Wolf 59]

Speakers of Nuuchahnulth have a strong disinclination to use clauses that contain more than one overt argument. This reluctance sometimes prompts speakers to express a single participant in two successive clauses. In (190) the overt subject *ƛaʔuukʷiʔatḥ* 'Clayoquot' and object *minwaaʔathʔi* 'the British soldiers' are distributed over two clauses based on the same predicate *hinaačiƛ* '(they) went out to sea to meet'; (191) illustrates the same phenomenon.

(190)

hinaačiʔaƛ	***ƛaʔuukʷiʔatḥ.***
hin -a·či(ƛ) -'aƛ	*ƛaʔu:kʷiʔatḥ*
get.there -going.out.to.meet -TEL	Clayoquot
went.out.to.meet	Clayoquot

hinaačiƛ	***minwaaʔathʔi.***
hin -a·či(ƛ)	*minwa:ʔath -ʔi·*
get.there -going.out.to.meet	British.soldiers -DEF
went.out.to.meet	the.British.soldiers

'Clayoquots went [in their canoes] out to sea to meet the British soldiers.' [Kingfisher 204]

(191)

sukʷiƛ	***ḥaw̓iłuk***	***ƛaʔuukʷiʔatḥ.***
sukʷi(ƛ)	*ḥaw̓ił -uk*	*ƛaʔu:kʷiʔatḥ*
take	chief -POSS	Clayoquot
take	their.chief	Clayoquot

...

sukʷiƛ	***miimixt***
sukʷi(ƛ)	*mi:mixt*
take	NAME
take	

'The Clayoquot chief took Miimixt.' [Kingfisher 208]

In addition to the lack of internal complexity within the domain, the clause in Nuuchahnulth plays a very different role in the organization of discourse than it does in

English. In English the clause seems to correspond well to the event or state in discourse, and therefore it plays an important role in information packaging. In Nuuchahnulth, on the other hand, the domain defined by a predicate and its argument has a much less direct connection to the event structure. The predicate-argument cluster is often further combined with other predicate-argument clusters to form the predication of a single unitary event or state (see SERIALIZATION in section 4.4.2.1). In this respect the clause in Nuuchahnulth is more comparable to the 'clause' in serial verb languages than to the clause in English. In Nuuchahnulth the most active interaction between structural packaging and information packaging occurs in the domain of predication (see below) rather than at the clause level.

Considering the fact that the predicate-argument cluster in Nuuchahnulth does not show many of the structural and functional characteristics observed with the domain of clause in English and other widely studied European languages, it may be misleading to call it 'clause'. In this work, nevertheless, the term 'clause' is adopted for the sake of familiarity and comparability. Readers with typological interests are especially urged to note the fundamental differences in the domain of the 'clause' in Nuuchahnulth and that of the clause in European languages. One should be careful about equating these domains on the basis of the labels used here.

4.2.2. The Phrase

A PHRASE is a domain consisting of a nominal or verbal head and its modifiers. It is defined by three coinciding structural patterns: (1) generally PHRASES are not interrupted by intonational breaks; (2) the word order of the modifiers in a PHRASE is mostly fixed, unlike the word order of predicative words beyond the domain of the PHRASE (see section 4.4.2.1 on SERIALIZATION); (3) a PHRASE can serve as a domain of suffixation.

4.2.2.1. Nominal phrase

A nominal phrase is formed with a nominal head and its modifying elements. It is relatively rare to have a nominal phrase with more than one modifying element in naturally occurring discourse. When multiple modifying expressions do co-occur, they appear in the following order: quantifier, numerals > property concepts > nominal. The order among these modifying expressions is fixed.

(192) *ʔayiips*			*ʔaʔiiḥ*	*muwač*
ʔaya	*-i·p*	*-s*	*ʔaʔi:ḥʷ*	*muwač*
many	-getting	-1sg	large	deer

'I got many big deer.' [elicited CL 99.08.15-16]

(193) *ˀaƛciqisˀiš* *tupqumɬ* *č̓apac.*
ˀaƛ-ciq *-ʿis* *-ˀi·š* *tup* *-qumɬ* *č̓apac*
two -being.on.the.shore? -being.on.the.beach -IND.3 black -all.over canoe
'There are two black canoes on the beach.' [elicited CL 99.8.15-22]

A nominal phrase can be the domain of lexical suffixation. When lexical suffixes are semantically associated with a phrase, they are invariably attached to the first constituent of the phrase regardless of the semantic head. This is illustrated in (194)–(196) below: the lexical suffix *-i·ɬ* 'making' is attached to the first constituent of the phrase regardless of the semantic head of that phrase *č̓apac* 'canoe' in these examples.

(194) *č̓aapaciiɬ*
č̓apac ***-i·ɬ***
canoe -making
'He made a canoe.' [elicited GL]

(195) *ƛuɬiiɬ* *č̓apac*
ƛuɬ ***-i·ɬ*** *č̓apac*
nice -making canoe
'He made a nice canoe.' [elicited CL]

(196) *ˀiiḥiiɬ* *ƛuɬ* *č̓apac*
ˀi·ḥ ***-i·ɬ*** *ƛuɬ* *č̓apac*
greatly -making nice canoe
'He made a very nice canoe.' [elicited CL]

The fact that the suffix *-i·ɬ* 'making' shifts its host in (194) through (196) suggests that its placement is not based on the inherent semantic or morphosyntactic properties of the individual elements in the phrase. Instead, it is determined dynamically on the basis of the structural arrangement of the elements within the syntactic complex. In a sense, lexical suffixes are associated with the complex as a whole rather than with any individual element within the complex.[2] This domain phenomenon with respect to suffixation justifies a recognition of the phrase in Nuuchahnulth.

---

[2] The exact nature of the association of lexical suffixes with the syntactically complex expression is an interesting issue. The way the lexical suffix changes its host is strongly reminiscent of the behavior of clitics. This analysis, however, is typologically rather odd. Crosslinguistically, clitics are typically found among grammatical morphemes that have more general, abstract functions. Lexical suffixes, however, have relatively concrete lexical meanings, and consequently their subcategorization frames are fairly specific. The clitic view, therefore, does not stand as a very plausible analysis. Moreover, the host-changing behavior of lexical suffixes in Nuuchahnulth is not necessarily similar to the mechanical migration found in cliticization. Thus, the association of lexical suffixes with a phrase is not characterized as cliticization. See section 2.4.2.1 for a detailed discussion of the issue.

Peripheral suffixes show the same attachment pattern with respect to the nominal phrase: when a nominal phrase occurs as a predicate, placement of peripheral suffixes is mostly on the first word, and word order is mostly inflexible. For example, observe the expression *muuˀaƛquu maˀayił* 'four families' in (197). The MOOD suffix *-qu:* CONDITIONAL (third person) is attached to the first word, and the order between *muu* 'four' and *maˀayił* 'family' cannot be reversed.

(197) *muuˀaƛquu* *maˀayił hiił.*
mu: -'aƛ ***-qu:*** *maˀayił hi:ł*
four -TEL -COND.3 family be.there.in.a.house
'There used to be four families living in the house.' [CLLS 34]

Similarly, in (198) the MOOD suffix *-ˀi·š* INDICATIVE (third person) is attached to the first word, and the order between *ṗišaq* 'bad' and *ˀiiqḥy̓ak* 'news' cannot be reversed.

(198) *ṗišaqˀiš* *ˀiiqḥy̓ak.*
ṗišaq ***-ˀi·š*** *ˀi:qḥ -y̓ak*
bad -IND.3 tell -instrument
'There is bad news.' [Kingfisher 98]

Attachment of the DEFINITE suffix *-ˀi·* follows the same pattern. As illustrated in the following examples, *-ˀi·* is attached to the modifying expression rather than the nominal.

(199) ***ˀučknaḥˀisˀi,*** *kuukuḥw̓isa*
ˀunaḥ -<čk>-ˀis ***-ˀi·*** *ku:kuḥw̓isa*
size -DIM -DIM -DEF hair.seal
'the small hair seal' [Qawiqaalth 18]

(200) ***čamiḥtaˀi*** *qʷayac̓iik*
čamiḥta ***-ˀi·*** *qʷayac̓i:k*
proper -DEF wolf
'the real wolves' [Mink 224]

(201) ***ƛułaqakˀi*** *ḥaakʷaaƛ*
ƛuł -aq -ak ***-ˀi·*** *ḥa:kʷa:ƛ*
nice -very -DUR -DEF girl
'the very beautiful girl' [Mink 287]

4.2.2.2. Verbal Phrase

In a verbal phrase the modifying word typically precedes the verbal head.

(202) *ˀiiḥwaaˀiš ta*ˀ*ił.*
*ˀi:ḥʷ-**wa·ˀi·š*** *taˀił*
very -QUOT.3 sick
'[They say] he is very sick.' [elicited CL 94.7.8-84]

Suffixation on a verbal phrase shows the same unusual pattern that is observed with respect to a nominal phrase: peripheral suffixes attach to the first word within the verbal phrase.

(203)

a. *taˀiłwaaˀiš.*
taˀił ***-wa·ˀi·š***
sick -QUOT.3
'[They say] he is sick.'

b. *ˀiiḥwaaˀiš taˀił.*
*ˀi:ḥʷ-**wa·ˀi·š*** *taˀił*
very -QUOT.3 sick
'[They say) he is very sick.'

In Nuuchahnulth modifying words like *ˀi:ḥʷ* 'very' cannot be clearly distinguished from other 'full-fledged' predicative words. This fact makes the verbal phrase appear similar to serialization, as in (204):

(204) *huuˀakmaḥsat wałyaqpiˀat*
hu:ˀak-maḥsa -'at wał -yaq -pi(ƛ) -'at
early -wanting.to -PASS go.home -having.done -MOM -PASS
'You would want to go home early.' [Canoe 93]

Structurally, both the verbal phrase and serialization consist of multiple predicative words combined to express some unitary meaning. However, despite the similarity in structural makeup, the verbal phrase and serialization represent different types of syntactic domains. First, the verbal phrase seems to have a fairly clear semantic head (i.e., the semantic contribution of one predicative word is limited to restricting the interpretation of the other predicative word), whereas there is no clear semantic head in serialization. Second, the word order is fixed in the verbal phrase but not in serialization. In the prototypical verbal phrase the combined predicative word expresses a highly abstract modificational meaning and has a scope that is highly localized to the verbal head rather than spread over the whole predication. The modifying word *ˀi:ḥʷ* 'very' is a good example of a predicative word with an abstract meaning and a clear localized scope.

4.2.2.3. The Nature of the Domain

It is probably overstructuralization to consider the phrase a purely structural domain. The fixed word order and the clitic-like suffixation pattern seem to provide a reasonable justification for the recognition of the PHRASE domain, but they do not necessarily suggest that the domain is purely structural. In fact, both features of the domain seem to come from the semantic scope relationship among the words. Thus, although the domain of a phrase plays a relevant role in structural organization in Nuuchahnulth, it should not be taken as a domain that can be defined in purely structural terms.

4.2.3. Predication

PREDICATION is a domain for expressing a single state of affairs (event or state). A PREDICATION contains only one predicate with peripheral suffixes, although it may consist of more than one predicative word. Note that the presence of an inflected predicate does not necessarily constitute a defining characteristic of PREDICATION. Predication-level peripheral suffixes are often omitted, especially in continuous discourse. (See below for further discussion of 'finiteness' in Nuuchahnulth.)

Predication-level peripheral suffixes are those that are sensitive to the properties of predication. They include suffixes indicating mood, the person and number of the subject, and tense. These suffixes show characteristics of 'inflection': (i) they always follow derivational suffixes (lexical, causative, and PERSPECTIVE-SHIFTING suffixes), (ii) they can be attached to any predicate regardless of its semantic properties, (iii) their meanings/functions are highly abstract or grammaticized, and (iv) they form paradigmatic sets. But, unlike typical inflectional suffixes, they are not structurally obligatory. Although there is variation in the degree of obligatoriness, from mostly obligatory person suffixes to mostly absent tense suffixes, none of these suffixes are 'structurally obligatory' in the sense that the lack of them automatically leads to an ungrammatical form. Thus, to the extent that structural obligatoriness is a defining characteristic of inflectional suffixes crosslinguistically, it is questionable whether it is appropriate to call the mood, person, and tense suffixes in Nuuchahnulth 'inflectional'. This issue, however, is extrinsic to the internal organization of Nuuchahnulth grammar.

The nature of the predication-level peripheral suffixes has direct implications for the status of the widely used notion of 'finiteness' in Nuuchahnulth grammar. Traditionally, the notion of finiteness has played an important role in accounting for various aspects of syntactic structuring. However, the concept of finiteness in its most idealized form is not very useful as a structural notion in Nuuchahnulth grammar.

Finiteness is typically defined on the basis of morphological completeness and syntactic independence: that is, a 'finite' verb has all the verbal morphological trappings and is used in a syntactically independent clause. But there are two major difficulties in applying the notion to predicates in Nuuchahnulth.

First, we cannot dichotomize predicative forms into exclusive categories of fully inflected and inflection-less forms. As pointed out above, predication-level peripheral suffixes are not structurally obligatory, nor do they always co-occur: that is, the predicate can occur with some peripheral suffixes but not with others. Consequently, predicative words can be inflected to varying degrees. Thus, it is more meaningful to talk about density of inflectional marking than just its presence or absence.

Second, the connection between morphological 'finiteness' and syntactic 'finiteness' is neither self-evident nor meaningful in Nuuchahnulth. In languages where inflectional suffixes can be considered structurally obligatory, i.e., where inflectional suffixes are required in a structurally definable domain, it is plausible to consider inflectionally incomplete forms to be 'structurally dependent'. In such languages, it is not possible to omit inflectional markers for nonstructural reasons, e.g., because they are inferable from context. Compare this with the situation in Nuuchahnulth. Distribution of inflectional markings is not completely bound to any structurally definable domain and can be absent for nonstructural reasons. In particular, zero mood and tense markings are so pervasive that it is unreasonable to give a structural characterization of the distribution of these markers. Thus, the functional role of the finite form in Nuuchahnulth seems to be very different from that in languages where nonfinite forms show a very limited and structured distribution pattern. Informal scanning of Nuuchahnulth narrative texts suggests that the peaks of inflectional density are found at major narrative scene boundaries, in narrator's comments, and in climactic parts of the narratives.

The domain of PREDICATION in Nuuchahnulth shows some functional characteristics that can be compared to those of the domain of clause in English. PREDICATION, like the clause in English, serves as the domain of event packaging. However, the structural characteristics of PREDICATION are very different from the domain of clause in English. One difference is that a predication can consist of multiple predicate-argument clusters. Another point of difference is that the predication in Nuuchahnulth as a structural domain does not show the structural rigidity of English clauses. The clause in English represents a fairly tight and robust unit of syntactic organization, although the tightness and robustness of the unit are often overemphasized, especially in formal approaches to grammar. This structural tightness and robustness can be evidenced in the highly elaborate and rigid lexical and syntactic categories distinguished within the domain: these categories represent strong functional and structural specialization within the clause. In Nuuchahnulth such strong functional and structural specialization and rigidification are not observed in the domain of PREDICATION. (See a related discussion in section 4.4.2.1 concerning the notion of 'prepositional clause'.)

As mentioned above, a predication can consist of one or more predicate-argument clusters, or clauses. When it consists of multiple clauses, these clauses share the same mood, tense, and often subject. Suffixes indicating the shared mood, tense, and subject are normally found only on the first predicate, other predicates being left unmarked for these values. (For further detailed discussion see section 4.4.2.1 on SERIALIZATION.)

(205)	*ˀacyuuˀaƛquuč*					*ˀuˀuˀiiḥ*		*ƛiḥapiiḥ.*
	ˀac	*-yu·*	*-'aƛ*	***-qu:***	*-č*	*ˀu*	*-'i:ḥ*	*ƛiḥapi:ḥ*
	go.out.fishing	-done	-TEL	-COND.3	-INF	it	-hunting	red.snapper
	would.be.out.for.food					gathering		red.snapper

'He would go out fishing for red snapper.' [GLLS 68]

(206)	*huuˀakˀaƛquus*			*mamuuk.*
	hu:ˀak-	*'aƛ*	***-qu:s***	*mamu:k*
	early	-TEL	-COND.1sg	work
	I.would.do.early			work

'I would work early.' [GLLS 147]

(207)	*šiƛkʷisaƛna*				*maaqtusiis*	*histaqšiƛ.*		
	šiƛ	*-kʷisa*	*-'aƛ*	***-na·***	*ma:qtusi:s*	*his*	*-taq*	*-ši(ƛ)*
	move	-moving.away.from	-TEL	-1pl	NAME	get.there	-coming.from	-MOM
	we.moved.away.from				NAME	came.from		

'We moved from Maaqtusiis.' [CLLS 232]

Since a predication contains only one predicate marked with predication-level peripheral suffixes, it should be possible in theory to unambiguously identify boundaries of predications on the basis of the presence and absence of the predication-level suffixes. However, in practice the morphological richness does not provide as definitive a demarcation of a predication as one might expect. In actual discourse, especially in narratives, forms without any mood suffix, 'absolutive forms', are used extensively, as noted above, and the pronominal suffix for the most frequent subject in narratives, i.e., the third person, is zero. Consequently, there is frequent indeterminacy as to whether a combination of predicates forms a single predication or two separate ones. (See Jacobsen 1993: 240 for a comparable observation.) Observe the following example:

(208)	*siikaa*		*hitačinƛ*		*maaqtusiis.*
	si:k	*-(y)a·*	*hita*	*-činƛ*	*ma:qtusi:s*
	sal	-CONT	get.there	-getting.into.a.bay	NAME
	sailing		entered.into.a.bay		NAME
	PREDICATE 1		**PREDICATE 2**		

'They sailed into the bay of Maaqtusiis.' [Kingfisher 2]

On the basis of morphological characteristics it is difficult to determine whether *siikaa* 'sailing' and *ḥitac̓inƛ maaqtusiis* 'entering the bay of Maaqtusiis' constitute separate predications or a single complex predication. There is similar indeterminacy in (209) with respect to the two predicates *c̓iiqaaʔaƛquuč* 'used to sing songs' and *ʔaatḥšiƛ* 'became night'.

(209)	*c̓iiqaaʔaƛquuč*	*ʔaatḥšiƛ.*
	c̓i:q-(y)a·-'aƛ -qu: -č	*ʔatḥ -ši(ƛ)*
	sing -CONT -TEL -COND.3 -INF	night -GRAD
	used.to.sing.songs	becoming.night

'He used to sing his song at night.' [Wolf 68]

Furthermore, when a predication consists of multiple clauses, there is a question about the relationship between the argument structure of each predicate and the configuration of arguments in relation to the combined predicate. For example, *quuquuʔas* 'people, humans' in the following sentence is a syntactic argument of the predicate *ʔuukʷił* 'doing to, with reference to', but at the same time it seems to be semantically associated with the predicate *naʔaackʷi* 'understood'.

(210)	*naʔaackʷi*	*qʷayac̓iik*	*ʔuukʷił*	***quuquuʔas,***
	naʔa: -ckʷi·	*qʷayac̓i:k*	*ʔu -kʷił*	*DUP- qu:ʔas*
	hear -happened	wolf	it -doing.to	DISTR- man
	understood	wolf	to.him	people

'Wolves understood what humans were saying.' [Wolf 38]

However, despite the semantic tie, there is no solid foundation for recognizing a direct syntactic relationship between a predicate and an argument that belong to different clauses. Thus, structural argumenthood can be defined only in relation to a single predicate, and in that sense the locus of argumenthood is the domain of the clause.

4.3. Argument Structure

This section presents various aspects of the configuration of participants in a predication. Given the semantic content of a predicate, participants involved in the event or state can often be anticipated. The configuration of participants in relation to the predicate has often been discussed under the term 'argument structure' or 'subcategorization frame'. Depending on what one takes to be the basis of association it is possible to speak of the pairing of the predicate and its associated participants in more than one way, and it is therefore important to be clear about different dimensions of such association. This work distinguishes two dimensions of the predicate-participant association, calling one

ARGUMENT STRUCTURE and the other PARTICIPANT STRUCTURE. ARGUMENT STRUCTURE refers to the configuration of participants that are syntactically in direct relationships with the predicate. PARTICIPANT STRUCTURE refers to the discourse-pragmatic configuration of participants within an event expressed by the predication. Since PARTICIPANT STRUCTURE refers to an abstract configuration of participants (i.e., one not bound by grammatical structure), the actual structural makeup of the domain of PARTICIPANT STRUCTURE can vary.

Observe example (211) below. The participants, *ˀumˀiiqsuˀi* 'the mother' and *kuukuḥẇisa* 'hair seal', are in a direct syntactic relationship, i.e., one without any syntactic mediation, with the predicate *wiḥisaňap* 'bring up ashore', and thus are considered to be part of the ARGUMENT STRUCTURE of the predicate.

(211)	*wiḥisaňap*		***ˀumˀiiqsuˀi,***	***kuukuḥẇisa*****.**
	wiḥi	*-'saňap*	*ˀumˀi·qsu -ˀi·*	*ku:kuḥẇisa*
	be.on.dry.land	-placing.on.the.beach	mother -DEF	hair.seal
	bringing.up.ashore		the.mother	hair.seal
	PREDICATE		**PARTICIPANT**	**PARTICIPANT**

'The mother brought hair seals up to the bank.' [Qawiqaalth 144]

At the same time, the participants in this example are part of the PARTICIPANT STRUCTURE of the predication '*the mother brought hair seals up to the bank*' based on the predicate '*bringing up ashore*', since they are discourse-pragmatically associated with the predicate to make up the event.

Although the need for distinguishing ARGUMENT STRUCTURE and PARTICIPANT STRUCTURE may not be obvious in a case like (211), the distinction is very useful when a predication involves a combination of multiple predicate-argument sets as illustrated in (212). Example (212) is a single predication, but it contains multiple clauses.

(212)	*ƛaapsˀatu*	*qawiqaaɬ,*	*tukuuk*	*ˀukʷink.*
	ƛaps -ˀatu	*qawiqa:ɬ*	*tuku:k*	*ˀu -kʷink*
	dive -sinking.into.water	Qawiqaalth	sea.lion	it -being.together.with
	dive.into.water	Qawiqaalth	sea.lion	be.together.with.it

'Qawiqaalth dove into the sea with the sea lion.' [Qawiqaalth 171]

Here we can speak of two separate ARGUMENT STRUCTURES based on two predicates: i.e., one between *ƛaapsˀatu* 'dive into the water' and *qawiqaaɬ* 'Qawiqaalth' (personal name); the other between *ˀukʷink* 'make it' and *tukuuk* 'sea lion'.

(212')	*ɬaapsˀatu*	*qawiqaaɬ,*	*tukuuk*	*ˀukʷink.*
	ɬaps -ˀatu	*qawiqa:ɬ*	*tuku:k*	*ˀu -kʷink*
	dive -sinking.into.water	Qawiqaalth	sea.lion	it -being.together.with
	dive.into.water	Qawiqaalth	sea.lion	be.together.with.it
	← ARG STRUCT 1 →		← ARG STRUCT 2 →	

The relationship between *ɬaapsˀatu* 'dive into the water' and *tukuuk* 'sea lion', however, is basically interpretive and cannot be considered part of the structurally defined ARGUMENT STRUCTURE of *ɬaapsˀatu* 'dive into the water'. On the other hand, in terms of the PARTICIPANT STRUCTURE, i.e., the discourse-pragmatic configuration of the participants within an event, *qawiqaaɬ* 'Qawiqaalth' and *tukuuk* 'sea lion' are part of the same participant configuration. Thus, the ARGUMENT STRUCTURE of the predicate(s) has implications for, and sometimes determines, the PARTICIPANT STRUCTURE within the predication, but they are not the same.

There is some doubt as to whether we should speak of a unitary complex structural configuration, as well as a discourse-semantic configuration with predications having multiple predicates.[3] Because of semantic unity, it is tempting to compare Nuuchahnulth complex predications and verb serializing in many languages to a complex clause with prepositional or adverbial phrases in English. However, it does not seem appropriate to equate the two. Within the complex predication, only one predicate can bear predication-level peripheral suffixes. This fact certainly suggests that the predication forms a structural domain with respect to peripheral suffixation. However, it does not necessarily follow that arguments around multiple predicates are structurally merged and integrated into a tight configuration comparable to the English clause with its various phrases. In English clauses, highly specialized and grammaticized elements are interlockingly combined to form an integral structure. However, predicates constituting a complex predication in Nuuchahnulth are far less structurally specialized. They are more loosely combined (without strict structural selection restrictions) than the elements in an English clause. Therefore, it is not appropriate to equate the structure of a complex predication in Nuuchahnulth to an English clause with multiple phrases.

4.3.1. Argument Structure in Nuuchahnulth

In traditional Western linguistics the notion of argument structure has been associated with a domain comparable to PREDICATION. This has been possible because the domain of the structural configuration of participants and that of the discourse-pragmatic configuration of participants show a significant overlap in realization and a consequent

[3] This issue is parallel to the controversy concerning the nature of the participant configuration in serial verb constructions that are found in languages of Africa, Austronesia, and Asia (see Foley and Olson 1985; Pawley 1987, 1993; Durie 1997).

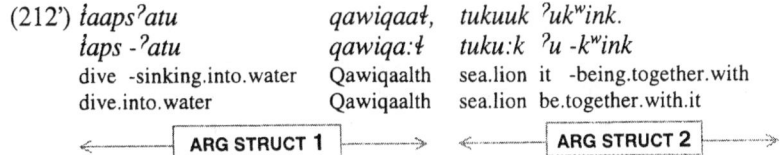

dense interaction between the two domains. What serves as a structural stage for that interaction is the clause. The clause is a highly grammaticized unit formed around a single predicate. Within the clause all the participants can be considered structurally associated with, and therefore part of the argument structure of, the predicate. The clause, at the same time, tends to correspond to a discourse unit of event. This close association between the structural ARGUMENT STRUCTURE and the discourse-pragmatic PARTICIPANT STRUCTURE via the unit of the clause has made it possible to study the direct interaction between grammatical characteristics and discourse characteristics of the participants: e.g., characterizations of 'subject' vs. 'object', or 'core' vs. 'oblique' in terms of semantic or discourse characteristics of participants typically associated with these grammatical roles. Note that although this type of research has been done widely, this association between the structural ARGUMENT STRUCTURE and the discourse-pragmatic PARTICIPANT STRUCTURE is not necessarily given crosslinguistically and has to be examined and established on the basis of the structural trends in each language. In Nuuchahnulth, a single event, and consequently a single discourse-pragmatic PARTICIPANT STRUCTURE, can be expressed with a combination of multiple clauses. In other words, the domain of ARGUMENT STRUCTURE formation and that of PARTICIPANT STRUCTURE formation do not always match. Thus, in Nuuchahnulth there is not as direct an interaction between the ARGUMENT STRUCTURE and PARTICIPANT STRUCTURE as that found, for example, in English. Consequently, we should not expect to be able to make a direct comparison between Nuuchahnulth and English in terms of interaction between grammatical characteristics and discourse characteristics of the participants. Thus, in a typologically valid discussion of argument structure we need to recognize variability in terms of the structural and functional environment surrounding the argument structure.

4.3.2. Characteristics of Arguments in Nuuchahnulth

4.3.2.1. Subjects

The SUBJECT in Nuuchahnulth can be distinguished from other direct arguments mainly in terms of morphological and functional characteristics: the subject is an argument, the person and number of which are indexed on the predicate, and it is more topical (see Givón 1984) than other arguments. Although morphological characteristics serve as reliable criteria for the identification of SUBJECT, it should be noted that the marking of the person and number in Nuuchahnulth is not structurally obligatory (see sections 2.4.3.1 and 2.4.3.2.11).

The category of SUBJECT is also relevant in syntactic organization. For example, some complement-taking predicates require the subject of a complement clause to be coreferential with the matrix subject.

(213)[4] [Rose 1981 p.87: 231]

a. matrix subj.= *I* ; complement subj.=*I*

ňamaɬšƛ̓intiis	***ˀuˀaaƛ̓***	*Joe*
ňamaɬ-ši(ƛ̓)-int -(y)i:s	*ˀu -'i(ƛ̓) -'aƛ̓*	
try -MOM -PAST -INDF.1sg	it -inviting -TEL	
I.tried	invited.him	

'I tried to invite Joe.'

b. matrix subj.= *I* ; complement subj.=*someone*

**ňamaɬšƛ̓intiis*	***ˀuˀaaƛ̓***	*siičiɬ*
ňamaɬ-ši(ƛ̓)-int -(y)i:s	*ˀu -'i(ƛ̓) -'aƛ̓*	*si: -(č)iɬ*
try -MOM -PAST -INDF.1sg	it -inviting -TEL	I -doing.to...
I.tried	invited.him	me

Intended as: 'I tried for someone to invite me.'

There is no denying that the category of subject is useful in capturing patterns and constraints in syntactic organization, but it does not necessarily follow that subject in Nuuchahnulth is a 'syntactic category' or some sort of syntactic primitive. The coreferentiality constraint may very well be viewed as a pragmatic constraint on perspective consistency between the matrix and complement clauses; and the 'subject category' (seen in the syntactic patterning) is really pragmatic rather than syntactic in nature. In fact, this latter pragmatic view seems to capture better the true nature of the phenomenon. In Nuuchahnulth there is no process that manipulates the syntactic arrangement of clausal arguments per se, nor is it possible to identify a syntactic slot that is clearly privileged in purely syntactic terms. Thus, there is not a strong structural motivation for purely syntactic categories in Nuuchahnulth. (See Whistler 1985 for a similar observation.)

4.3.2.2. Objects

In a predication with more than one argument, only the subject is positively identified with a grammatical marker in Nuuchahnulth.[5] The only exception is in the imperative mood suffixes where not only the person and number of subject but also those of a nonsubject argument is indicated.

---

[4] Although the examples cited here are from a northern dialect Kyuquot, the point made here is not affected by the dialectal differences.

[5] The object, as well as the subject, is indicated in the pronominal suffixes in the related languages Ditidaht and Makah (see Klokeid 1976; Jacobsen 1973).

(214) *naaʔuuqstaʔičin*
naʔu· *-'a·qsta* ***-'i·čin***
accompany -being.amongst-IMP.2p>1p
'Join us.' [CLLS 269]

Thus, the pattern in the imperative mood paradigm provides the basis, although rather limited, for recognizing a structural entity that is separate from the subject. Given the structural and functional similarity to the object in other languages, it seems reasonable to term the entity 'object'.

When the predicate can take more than one nonsubject participant — typically a recipient and a patient — it is the person and number of the recipient that are indicated in the imperative suffix. In (215) the imperative suffix only indicates the person and number of the recipient, first-person singular, and not those of the patient *water*, third-person singular.

(215) *č̓aʔak ʔuyiiʔis*
č̓aʔak ʔu -yi· ***-'i·s***
water it -giving **-IMP.2s>1s**
'Give me water.' [Lesson 7]

Thus, when there is more than one nonsubject direct argument, only one of them, the recipient in (215), is the object. We can therefore distinguish the object and nonobject among nonsubject direct arguments. This distinction seems straightforward in theory. However, in practice the distinction is often difficult to determine. Note that the imperative mood paradigm by itself is of rather limited use as a general structural test for objecthood: there are many predicates that are semantically incompatible with the imperative mood. Unfortunately, there do not seem to be other structural patterns that clearly corroborate the definition of object based on the pattern of the imperative mood paradigm.[6] Consequently, the distinction between object and nonobject is not very robust.

In this connection, it is interesting to note that the direct argument expressing agent in a predication having the PERSPECTIVE-SHIFTING suffix *-'at*. Without *-'at*, nonsubject arguments express a low-agency participant (such as patient or recipient) rather than a high-agency participant (such as agent); (216) and (217) provide typical examples. Both *qʷayaac̓ikm̓it* 'Son of Wolf' in (216) and *kuukuḥw̓isa* 'hair seal' in (217) are low in agency.

---

[6] Rose (1981: 57–61) argues that the distinction between object and nonobject (Rose's 'adjunct' and 'oblique') can be made based on word-order flexibility: the object can precede the predicate, whereas a nonobject cannot. This distinction is not borne out by my data.

(216)

ẏimqƛ̓	*č̓aastimcm̓it,*		***qʷayaac̓ikm̓it.***	
ẏimqƛ̓	*č̓a:stimc*	*-m̓i·t*	*qʷaya:c̓ik*	*-m̓i·t*
dislike	mink	-son.of	wolf	-son.of
	SUBJECT		**NONSUBJECT**	

'The Son of Mink didn't like the Son of Wolf.' [Mink 68]

(217)

ʔuʔinł		*kuukuḥw̓isa*	*qawiqaał.*
ʔu	*-'inł*	*ku:kuḥw̓isa*	*qawiqa:ł*
it	-giving.a.feast.of	hair.seal	Qawiqaalth
		NONSUBJECT	**SUBJECT**

'Qawiqaalth gave a feast of hair seal.' [Qawiqaalth 147]

However, in a predication with the PERSPECTIVE-SHIFTING suffix *-'at*, the high-agency participant can occur as a nonsubject argument. In the following examples, the high-agency participants, *Charlie Jones* and *qʷayac̓iikʔi* 'the wolf', are nonsubject arguments in that they do not control the pronominal suffix on the predicate.

(218)

waaʔaƛ̓ats				***Charlie Jones.***
wa:-'aƛ̓	*-'at*	*-s*		
say -TEL	-SHIFT	-1sg		
it.was.said.to.me				

'Charlie Jones said to me' [Canoe 120]

(219)

n̓aacsaats			***qʷayac̓iikʔi***	
n̓a:csa	*-'at*	*-s*	*qʷayac̓i:k*	*-ʔi·*
see	-SHIFT	-1sg	wolf	-DEF
watching.me			the.wolf	

'The wolf was watching me.' [Wolf 207]

Semantically these nonsubject participants are very different from prototypical objects. However, the predicate with PERSPECTIVE-SHIFTING suffix *-'at* can never be in the imperative mood, and therefore it is not possible to determine the status of the agent participant with respect to objecthood.

4.4. General Structure-Building Strategies

This section presents an overview of strategies employed in Nuuchahnulth to form internally complex constructions.

4.4.1. Expansion of Nominals

4.4.1.1. Nominal Concatenation

Nominal concatenation is an expansion strategy where two nominals are juxtaposed to express a single concept. In nominal concatenation one nominal functions as a modifier, as illustrated by *muwač* 'deer' in (220).

(220) *tiičma muwač*
heart deer
'deer heart' [Wolf 69]

(221) *ˁiniiƛ tiič*
dog life
'dog life' [Dog 26]

Nominal concatenation is not a common expansion strategy. In the collection of texts used in this project the above examples are the only instances of the construction. When presented in isolation, examples (220) and (221) above were not accepted by a younger (but fluent) speaker. Nor could any additional examples of the same construction be elicited from her. Rose (1981: 50f.) provides a description of a similar construction in Kyuquot.

4.4.1.2. Modification

MODIFICATION is a strategy of relating words where the function of one word is limited to restricting the interpretation of the other 'main' word. For example, in (222) and (223), *čamiḥtackʷi* 'having been respectable' and *ʔaya* 'many' modify the heads *ɬuucma* 'woman' and *ḥaaw̓iiḥaƛ* 'young men', respectively.

(222) ***čamiḥtackʷi*** *ɬuucma,*
čamiḥta -ckʷi· *ɬu:cma*
proper -happened woman
'She was an honorable woman.' [GLLS 23]

(223) ***ʔaya*** *ḥa:w̓i:ḥaƛ.*
ʔaya *ḥa:w̓i:ḥaƛ*
many young.men
'There were many young men.' [Qawiqaalth 31]

MODIFICATION represents a HEADED relationship in that the scope of the semantic contribution of the nonmain word is limited to the 'main' word. The nonhead does not affect the syntactic behavior of the complex as a whole, and therefore the behavioral characteristics of the whole complex reflect those of the head. Thus, in terms of syntactic behavior, the word serving as the head and the syntactic complex consisting of the head and nonhead words are equivalent.

4.4.1.2.1. Types of Modification

Depending on how modification interacts with the domain of PHRASE (see section 4.2.2), it is possible to distinguish two types of modification: INTEGRAL MODIFICATION and ADDITIVE MODIFICATION. In INTEGRAL MODIFICATION a modifier forms with the head an inseparable phrase unit in structural, as well as semantic and discourse, terms. Modifiers participating in the INTEGRAL MODIFICATION precede the head. In ADDITIVE MODIFICATION, on the other hand, modifiers do not participate in the domain phenomenon defining the phrase. The complex expanded by ADDITIVE MODIFICATION cannot serve as a base for lexical suffixation. The ADDITIVE modifiers are often separated from the head by an intonational boundary. In terms of ordering, they predominantly follow the head.

The type of modification strongly correlates with the internal complexity of the modifying expression. When the modifying expression consists of a single predicative word, as in the case of most expressions of quantities, quantificational concepts, and property concepts, it is likely to enter into INTEGRAL MODIFICATION. On the other hand, when the modifying expression consists of a predicative word and its argument, as in many expressions of actions, events, states, and locative concepts, it typically enters into ADDITIVE MODIFICATION.

4.4.1.2.2. General Organizational Principles

Although multiple modifying expressions rarely co-occur, when they do they occur in the following relative order:

NUMERAL	>	PROPERTY CONCEPT	>	NOMINAL	>	ACTION/EVENT/STATE
QUANTIFIER						LOCATIVE
QUALIFIER[7]						

[7] Qualifying expressions such as *ʔi:ḥʷ* 'very, greatly' are not directly associated with nominals but can appear within the nominal phrase as modifiers of property concepts.

Suffixes associated with a nominal complex expanded through integral modification, i.e., the phrase, are typically attached to the first modifying expression instead of the nominal head. This suffixation pattern is true with lexical suffixes and predicate-level peripheral suffixes. In (224) below the lexical suffix *-qs* 'in a vessel' is attached to the quantifying expression *ˀaya* 'many' instead of the nominal *tuškuuḥ* 'ling cod'.

(224) lexical suffix on a quantifying expression

ˀayaqsƛ̓a *tuškuuḥ.*
ˀaya **-qs** *-ƛ̓a·* *tušku:ḥ*
many -being.in.a.vessel -again ling.cod
QUANTIF. **NOMINAL**

'There was also plenty of cod in a canoe.'
'They also had many cod in the canoe.' [Qawiqaalth 145]

In (48) the lexical suffixes *-c̓as* 'being at the crown' and *-qi·* 'being on top' are attached to the numeral expression *ˀaƛ̓a* 'two' instead of the property concept *ƛ̓iḥuk* 'be red' or the nominal *ˁiyaał* 'feather'.

(225) lexical suffix on a numeral expression

ˀaƛ̓ac̓asqi **ƛ̓iḥuk** **ˁiyaał** *łuḥc̓iti,*
ˀaƛ̓a-**c̓as** **-qi·** *ƛ̓iḥ -uk* *ˁiya:ł* *łuḥc̓iti*
two -at.the.crown -on.top red -DUR feather head
NUMERAL **PROPERTY** **NOMINAL**

'There are two red feathers at the crown of his head.' [Canoe 13]

In (226) a predicative peripheral suffix *-ˀi·š* INDICATIVE third is associated with a nominal complex, and it is attached on the property concept *p̓išaq* 'be bad' instead of the nominal *ˀiiqḥy̓ak* 'news'.

(226) predicative inflection on a property concept

p̓išaqˀiš *ˀiiqḥy̓ak.*
p̓išaq **-ˀi·š** *ˀi:qḥ -y̓ak*
bad -IND.3 telling -instrument
PROPERTY **NOMINAL**

'There is bad news.' [Kingfisher 98]

4.4.1.2.3. Meanings Added through Modificational Expansion

Concepts that can be associated with a nominal through modification include quantifiers, quantities, qualifiers, property concepts, locations, actions, events, and states.

4.4.1.2.3.1. Quantifiers

Quantificational concepts such as *some*, *many*, or *all*, are typically expressed by a single-word modifier and precede a nominal.

(227) ***ˀaya*** *łaatḥaˀis* *ˀuušy̓aˀaƛquu*
ˀaya *ła:tḥa -ˀis* *ˀu:š -y̓a -'aƛ -qu:*
many children -DIM some -being.troubled.by -TEL -COND.3
MOD. **NOMINAL**
'Many children had a hard time [at school].' [GLLS 40]

4.4.1.2.3.2. Numerals

Numerals, whether they consist of a single word or multiple words, typically precede a nominal.

(228) ***muuˀaƛquu*** *maˀayiƚ* *hiiƚ.*
mu: *-'aƛ -qu:* *ma -ˀayiƚ* *hi:ƚ*
four -TEL -COND.3 dwell-being.in.a.house be.there.in.a.house
used.to.be.four families be.there.in.the.house
MODIFIER **NOMINAL**
'There used to be four families in the house.' [CLLS 34]

(229) ***ˀaƛaasˀaƛukqʷin*** *maƛimƚm̓inḥ.*
ˀaƛa *-a·s -'aƛ -uk -qʷin* *maƛ -imƚ -m̓inḥ*
two -being.on.a.surface-TEL -POSS -COND.1pl tied -rounded.object -PL
we.used.to.put.two.on.the.ground barrels
MODIFIER **NOMINAL**
'We used to put two barrels on the ground.' [CLLS 84]

(230) multiple-word numeral

ʔaƛpaaksa ḥaaw̓iiḥaƛ waa qacc̓a ḥaatḥaakʷaƛ.
ʔaƛpu -ʔa·k -sa ḥa:w̓i:ḥaƛ wa· qacc̓a ḥa:tḥa:kʷaƛ
seven -POSS -1sg sons and three daughters

waa ***caqiic ʔuḥʔiiš n̓upu*** *kʷakuuc,*
wa: caqi·c ʔuḥʔi:š n̓upu kʷaku:c
and twenty and six grandchildren
MODIFIER **NOMINAL**

'I have seven sons, three daughters, and twenty-six grandchildren ...' [CLLS 325]

4.4.1.2.3.3. Property Concepts

Property concepts typically precede a nominal.

(231) *ʔatquu* ***čamiḥta*** *quuʔas qawiqaał.*
ʔat -qu: čamiḥta qu:ʔas qawiqa:ł
even.if -COND.3 proper person Qawiqaalth
MODIFIER **NOMINAL**

'Although Qawiqaalth was a person with proper manners.' [Qawiqaalth 12]

(232) ***ʔaʔiiḥ*** *nuučyuu qacqasaƛquuč, ʔuušyuuya.*
ʔaʔi:ḥʷ nu:čyu: qacqas -'aƛ -qu: -č ʔu:š -yu:ya
large mountain.range disappear -TEL -COND.3 -INF some -being.at.the.time
MODIFIER **NOMINAL**

'Sometimes [sea lions would go so far away from the land that] large mountains would become out of sight.' [Qawiqaalth 106]

(233) *ʔucḥinƛ* ***ƛułaqakʔi*** *ḥaakʷaaƛ,*
ʔu -cḥi -in(ƛ) ƛuł-aq -ak -ʔi· ḥa:kʷa:ƛ
it -being.married.to -MOM nice -very -DUR -DEF girl
MODIFIER **NOMINAL**

'He got married to the very beautiful woman.' [Mink 287]

4.4.1.2.3.4. Event / State

Single-word modifiers qualifying an event or state typically precede the head nominal. These modifiers form a phrase with the head nominal in that they can form a single domain of suffixation with the nominal. In (234) and (235), the DEFINITE suffix *-ʔi·* is attached to the modifying expressions *maaṅuuˀisˀatḥiic* 'belonging to Manhousaht' and *ˀuusatukuk* 'making loud noise', respectively.

(234)	*naˀaaˀat*	***maaṅuuˀisˀatḥiicˀi***	*čiiqẏak.*
	naˀa:-'at	*ma:ṅu:ˀisˀatḥ-i:c* **-ˀi·**	*či:q-ẏak*
	hear -SHIFT	Manhousat -belonging.to-DEF	sing-instrument.for
	it.was.heard	one.belonging.to.Manhousats	song
		MODIFIER	**NOMINAL**

'They [Muchalats] heard Manhousat songs.' [Wolf 57]

(235)	*mamaɬṅi*	***ˀuusatukukˀi***	*mašiin,*
	ma -maɬ -ṅi·	*ˀu:sa -a·tuk -uk* **-ˀi·**	*maši:n*
	dwell -moving -coming	loud -making.sound.of -POSS -DEF	machine
	white.man	one.making.loud.noise	machine
		MODIFIER	**NOMINAL**

'white man's machine that makes loud noise' [Canoe 28]

Internally complex modifiers consisting of a predicative word and its argument generally follow the head nominal. These modifiers thus typically participate in additive modification: that is, the head nominal and the modifying expression do not form a phrase and therefore cannot serve as a unitary domain of suffixation. In the following examples, the head nominals *čistuup* 'rope' and *naniiqsakitqs* 'my late grandmother' are modified by *ṁuksẏu ˀuˀiḥta* 'having a stone at the end' and *ˀukɬaa muɬmuḥ* 'by the name of Multhmuh', respectively.

(236)	*taakšiˀat*	*ˀunaakˀat*	*čistuup*	***ṁuksẏu***	***ˀuˀiḥta.***
	ta:k -ši(ƛ)-'at	*ˀu -na·k -'at*	*čis -tu·p*	*ṁuksẏu*	*ˀu -'iḥta*
	always -MOM -SHIFT	it -having-SHIFT	rope-thing	stone	it -being.at.the.end
	it.is.always.done	one.has.it	rope	stone	at.the.end
				NOMINAL	**MODIFIER**

'You always use a rope with a stone at the end.' [Canoe 24]

(237)	*ˀuḥˀaƛatqʷin*	*naniiqsakitqs,*
	ˀuḥ -'aƛ -'at -qʷin	*nani·qsu -ˀa·k -it -qs*
	be.she -TEL -SHIFT -COND.1pl	grandparent -POSS -PAST -SUB.1sg
	it.was.she.who.did.to.us	my.late.grandmother
		NOMINAL
	ˀukɬaa muɬmuḥ,	*ˀuuˀaaɬukʷat.*
	ˀu -kɬa·	*ˀu -'a:ɬuk -'at*
	it -having.as.name NAME	it -looking.after -SHIFT
	being.named...	looking.after...
	MODIFIER	

'It used to be my late grandmother by the name of Multhmuh who looked after me.' [CLLS 16]

There are a few cases in my database of a complex modifying expression preceding the head nominal, but all of them are based on *ˀukɬaa* 'by the name of' as illustrated in example (238).

(238)	***qawiqaaɬ***	***ˀukɬaa***	*ḥaaw̓iɬaƛ.*
	qawiqa:ɬ	*ˀu -kɬa·*	*ḥa:w̓iɬaƛ*
	Qawiqaalth	it -having.as.name	young.man
	Qawiqaalth	being.named…	young.man
	MODIFIER		**NOMINAL**

'There was a young man named Qawiqaalth.' [Qawiqaalth 2]

This is probably because the expression NAME+*ˀukɬaa* 'by the name of' is conventionalized to the extent that it can be treated as a simple modifying expression much like a property concept. It is not clear at this point whether this use of NAME+*ˀukɬaa* is in an integral modification relationship to the nominal, since there is no example in my current database where a nominal complex with NAME+*ˀukɬaa* is associated with a lexical suffix, predication-level peripheral suffixes, or the DEFINITE suffix.

4.4.1.2.3.5. Location

Modifiers expressing locative notions often have a complex internal structure and generally follow the head nominal. These modifiers typically enter into additive modification.

(239)	*hiˀiisitwaˀiš*			*ˀiščiipm̓it*
	hiˀi:s	*-it*	*-wa·ˀi·š*	*ˀišči:p-m̓i·t*
	be.there.on.the.ground	-PAST	-QUOT.3	gum -son.of
	it.was.there			Son.of.Gum.Woman

nism̓aˀi	***hiɬ***	***ƛawaa***	***quḥaa,***
nism̓a -ˀi·	*hiɬ*	*ƛawa:*	*quḥa:*
land -DEF	be.there	near	NAME
the.land	be.there	near	Quhaa
NOMINAL		**MODIFIER**	

'Son of Gum Woman lived at the place near Qahaa' [GLLS 65]

(240)	*n̓aacsiičiƛwaˀiš*	*p̓aˤimˀi,*	***hiiɬapi***	***ḥaa***
	n̓a:csi: -či(ƛ) -wa·ˀi·š	*p̓aˤim -ˀi·*	*hiɬ -api*	*ḥa:*
	see -MOM -QUOT.3	limpet -DEF	be.there -being.up.in.the.air	there
	saw	the.limpet	hanging	there
		NOMINAL	**MODIFIER**	

'He saw limpets that were hanging from above.' [Mink 240]

(241) *hišumyiłʔaƛquuʔał* *hił*
hiš -umł -'ił -'aƛ -qu: -ʔa·ł *hił*
all -being.in.a.group -being.in.the.house -TEL -COND.3 -PL be.there
they.used.to.get.together be.there

cultural buildingʔakʔiʔał ***hiʔiis*** ***Sprout Lake.***
cultural building -ʔa·k -ʔi -ʔa·ł *hiʔi:s*
-POSS -??-PL be.there.on.the.ground
their.cultural.building be.there.on.the.ground
NOMINAL **MODIFIER**

'They would gather at their cultural building on Sprout Lake road.' [CLLS 270]

4.4.2. Expansion of Verbals

4.4.2.1. Serialization

SERIALIZATION[8] combines multiple clauses into a unit that expresses a single state of affairs (= event or state), i.e., a predication. (For a detailed discussion of PREDICATION see section 4.2.3.) In (242), *ʕuyaas* 'move' and *Alberni wałaak* 'go to Alberni' are both clauses, and they are combined to express a single event. Example (243) is a parallel example where a combination of two clauses *ʔuuščapanačaƛquu* 'used to go out' and *hiniic ʕiniiƛukʔi* 'bring their dogs' expresses a single event.

(242) *ʕuyaasaƛna* *Alberni wałaak,*
ʕuya:s -'aƛ -na· *Alberni wała:k*
move -TEL -1pl NAME go
we.moved NAME go
← CLAUSE → ← CLAUSE →
'We moved to [Port] Alberni.' [GLLS 135]

(243) *ʔuuščapanačaƛquu* *hiniic ʕiniiƛukʔi.*
ʔu:š -ca -panač -'aƛ -qu: *hini:c ʕini:ƛ -uk -ʔi·*
some -going.to -moving.about -TEL -COND.3 bring dog -POSS -DEF
would.go.out bring their.dogs
← CLAUSE → ← CLAUSE →
'People used to go out with their dogs.' [Dog 13]

---

8 The term SERIALIZATION readily reminds one of the serial verb construction found in Asian and African languages. The parallelism between Nuuchahnulth SERIALIZATION and the serial verb construction holds with respect to their association with a single event/state. However, the parallelism cannot be extended much further. SERIALIZATION in Nuuchahnulth seems to represent a more general strategy than the serial verb construction: it is used to express verbal negation, verbal qualification, and nominal modification, as well as complex verbal concepts.

SERIALIZATION is different from COMBINING (a combination of multiple predications) in that the latter represents a combination of multiple states of affairs. Compare the examples below.

(244) SERIALIZATION

mamuukšiƛna	*ˀuyi*	*February*
mamu:k -ši(ƛ)-na·	*ˀuyi*	
working -MOM -1pl	at.the.time	
we.worked	at.that.time	
← CLAUSE →	← CLAUSE →	

'We worked in February.' [GLLS 110]

(245) COMBINING

ḥayuqˀičḥˀaƛits	*qʷiyaakiis*	*qaḥšiƛ*	*ˀumˀiiqsu.*
ḥayu -qˀičḥ -'aƛ -it -s	*qʷiyu -ˀa·k -(y)i:s*	*qaḥ -ši(ƛ)*	*ˀumˀi·qsu*
ten -year -TEL -PAST -1sg	when -POSS -INDF.1sg	dead -MOM	mother
I.was.ten.years.old	when.mine.did	died	mother
← CLAUSE →	← CLAUSE →		

'I was ten years old when my mother died.' [CLLS 18]

The temporal notion in (244) in combination with *mamuukšiƛna* 'we worked' constitutes a single event, thus representing SERIALIZATION. In (245) the temporal notion is expressed as a separate event with a mood and participants independent of the other state of affairs *ḥayuqˀičḥˀaƛits* 'I was ten years old', and is thus a case of COMBINING.

The distinction between SERIALIZATION and COMBINING is a matter of the structure of the state of affairs. Here a discussion of the notion of 'state of affairs' is in order. The notion of 'state of affairs', in the sense that is relevant to this discussion, has to do with the way the speaker chooses to package a scene rather than with the inherent semantic structure of a scene. Scenes that are exactly the same in a semantic or truth-conditional sense, i.e., consisting of exactly the same set of participants, time, place, mood, etc., are not necessarily expressed in the same way by all speakers at all times. A speaker may very well choose to package a scene as a single state of affairs at one time and package the same scene as a combination of multiple states of affairs at another. To put it in another way, the speaker can choose to express the semantically same scene using SERIALIZATION in one case and COMBINING in another. It should be noted that the speaker's choice is governed by the discourse context. Thus, whether a scene is expressed through SERIALIZATION or COMBINING is not inherent in the makeup of the scene itself but in the flow of discourse.

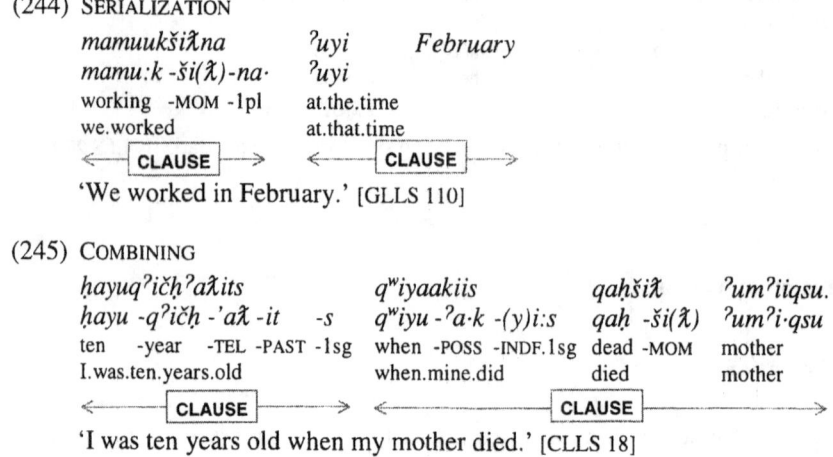

The way the definition of SERIALIZATION is formulated and the way SERIALIZATION and COMBINING are distinguished may suggest that the structure of the state of affairs (i.e., whether the scene is represented as a single state of affairs or a combination of multiple states of affairs, and also in the latter case how they are related to each other)

can be identified clearly and uncontroversially. In prototypical cases this is true: there are formal correlates with the structure of the state of affairs. Compare the following.

(246) SERIALIZATION

Roger	***ʔuʔukʷiłʔanitʔišʔaał***	***ʔuušyuuya,***
	DUP- *ʔu -kʷił -'at* ***-it*** *-ʔi·š -ʔa:ł*	*ʔu:š -yu:ya*
	DISTR- it -doing.to -SHIFT -PAST -IND.3 -always	some -at.the.time
	they.used.to.do.it.to.him	sometimes
←	CLAUSE 1 →	← CLAUSE 2 →

'Sometimes people called him Roger.' [GLLS 6]

(247) COMBINING

naʔaałanimts	***qʷiyuyiis***	*ʔaʔim*	*ƛiisƛiisšiƛ*
naʔa:ł -'at ***-imt*** *-s*	*qʷiyu -(y)i:s*	*ʔaʔim*	*ƛi:sƛi:s -ši(ƛ)*
understand -SHIFT -PAST -1sg	when -INDF.1sg	first.time	go.to.school -MOM
I.sort.of.understood	whenever.I	first.time	started.school
← PREDICATION 1 →	←	PREDICATION 2 →	

'I understood [English] when I first went to school.' [GLLS 42]

Within a complex consisting of serialized predicates as in (246), only the initial predicate *ʔuʔukʷiłʔat* 'they do it to him' will carry predication-level peripheral suffixes, if any. In contrast, in prototypical cases of COMBINING, each predicate combined carries predication-level suffixes even when there is an overlap of information, as in the predicates *naʔaałanimts* 'I understood' and *qʷiyuyiis* 'when I' in (247) (both predicates involve the first-person singular participant).

Unfortunately, this correlation between separateness of states of affairs and overt inflectional markings is not perfect. The presence of predication-level peripheral suffixes on a predicate unambiguously establishes the clause in question as a separate predication. Lack of them, however, does not necessarily serve as evidence that a given predicative expression does not constitute a separate predication, since predication-level peripheral suffixes are not structurally obligatory in predication-level structuring. (See Jacobsen 1993: 239f. for a similar observation.) Nevertheless, this does not necessarily invalidate the distinction between SERIALIZATION and COMBINING. The problem of structural indeterminacy involving forms without predication-level suffixes extends well beyond the distinction between SERIALIZATION and COMBINING and must be seen as part of the grammar of Nuuchahnulth (See the discussion on 'finiteness' in Nuuchahnulth in 4.2.3.)

4.4.2.1.1. Function of Serialization

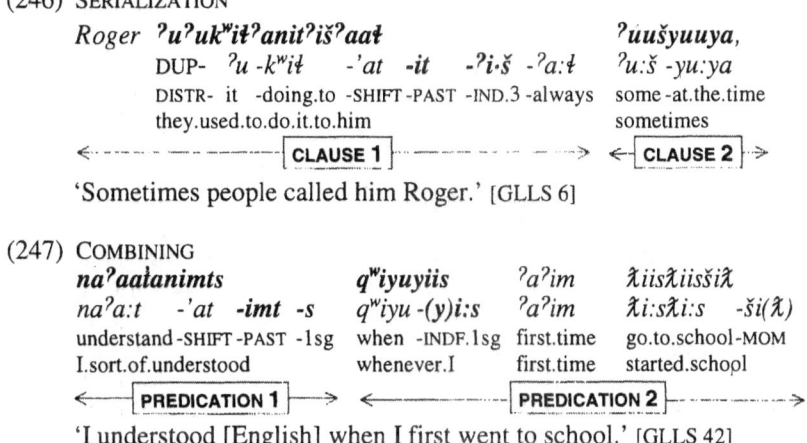

Serialization as an event-encoding strategy creates by combining predicates a complex predication that could not be expressed in a single word. It can form a predication that is informationally dense in terms of the event specification or in terms of the number of participants in an event. For example, in (248) the expression of an action *ƛawaˀiiˀaƛquuč* 'he would go near' is accompanied by a specification of manner *kʷaačiƛ* 'move backwards'. In (249) and (250), expressions of time and location, respectively, are accommodated.

(248) + manner

ƛawaˀiiˀaƛquuč	***kʷaačiƛ.***
ƛawa-ˀi: -'aƛ -qu: -č	*kʷa: -či(ƛ)*
near -reaching -TEL -COND.3 -INF	move.backwards-MOM
he.would.go.near	move.backwards

'[While he was dancing] he would go near [him] moving backwards.' [Mink 132]

(249) + time

qiis	*waɬyuu*
qi: -s	*waɬ -yu·*
for.long -1sg	go.home -done
I.for.long	at.home

'For a long time I stayed at home.' [GLLS 133]

(250) + location

yacaaqtuu	***ˀucačiƛ***	***ˀuuƛaqči.***
yac -a·qtu·	*ˀu -ca -či(ƛ)*	
step -going.over	it -going.to -MOM	NAME
walked.over.the.hill	went.there	Odlaqutla

'They went over [the high land] to Odlaqutla.' [Wolf 59]

The following examples illustrate the use of serialization to expand the number of participants accommodated in the predication. In (251) the predicate *hiisɫiƛ* 'take from' introduces the source *p̓atqsacˀisukˀi* 'his little bag' into the event *suxkʷiƛ ˤuy̓ic̓akˀi* 'taking his medicine bottle'. In (252) the predicate *ˀukʷink* 'together with' associates the comitative participant *tukuuk* 'sea lion' with the event *ɫaapsˀatu qawiqaaɫ* 'Qawiqaalth dove into the water'.

(251)

suxkʷiƛ	*ˤuy̓ic̓akˀi,*
sukʷi(ƛ) -<x>	*ˤuy̓i -c̓u· -ˀa·k -ˀi·*
take -MINK	medicine -being.inside.container -POSS -DEF
take	his.medicine.bottle

hiisɫiƛ	*ˀaḥ*	***p̓atqsacˀisukˀi.***
hist -'iƛ	*ˀaḥ*	*p̓atqʷ-sac -ˀis -uk -ˀi·*
get.there -taking	here	goods -receptacle -DIM -POSS -DEF
take.from	here	his.little.bag

'He took out his medicine bottle from this little bag of his.' [Mink 159]

(252)	*ł̓aapsˀatu*	*qawiqaał,*	***tukuuk***	***ˀukʷink.***
	ł̓aps -ˀatu	*qawiqa:ł*	*tuku:k*	*ˀu -kʷink*
	dive -sinking.into.water	Qawiqaalth	sea.lion	it -being.together.with
	dive.into.water	Qawiqaalth	sea.lion	together.with.it

'Qawiqaalth dove into the water with the sea lion.' [Qawiqaalth 171]

In such cases serialization provides a way to accommodate a larger amount of information in a predication.

Serialization is also used to accommodate an informationally dense participant structure. The information density within a clause is generally kept low: clauses with two overt participants are rare, especially when the two participants are both salient (= worth tracking) in discourse (see also 4.6.2 and 4.7.1 for a discussion on the number of overt participants observed in a clause). One common strategy for handling such an informationally dense participant structure is to spread the encoding of the event across serialized clauses, allowing each clause to carry only one discourse-salient participant. For example, compare (253) and (254). An event of *killing* can be expressed in a simple predication as in (253).

(253)	*qaḥsaapw̓ił̓as*	***č̓aastimcm̓it***	***ḥaw̓iłisimˀi,***
	qaḥ -sa·p -w̓ił̓as	*č̓a:stimc-m̓i·t*	*ḥaw̓iłisim -ˀi·*
	dead -MOMCAUS-about.to	mink -son.of	head.chief -DEF
	about.to.kill	Son.of.Mink	the.head.chief

'The Son of Mink is about to kill the leader of all.' [Mink 134]

Contrast this with the expression of a *killing* event in the following example. Example (254) occurs in the context in which the actor *Kwatyaat* and the victim *qʷayac̓iik* 'wolf' are presented as rivals, and thus in this confrontational situation both participants are highly salient. And this informationally dense participant structure is handled with serialized clauses. (See section 4.6.2 for more discussion on the relationship between the informational structure and sentence structure.)

(254)	*qaḥsaap̓aƛ̓*	***kʷatyaat***	*ˀuukʷił*	***qʷayac̓iik***
	qaḥ-sa·p -'aƛ̓		*ˀu -(č)ił*	*qʷayac̓i:k*
	die -MOMCAUS-TEL	NAME	it -doing.to	wolf
	killed		doing.to.it	wolf
	← CLAUSE →		← CLAUSE →	

'Kwatyaat killed Wolf.' (Sapir and Swadesh 1939: 30 ln. 5–6)

Notice that the semantic content of the predicate *qaḥsaap* 'kill' and the combination of *qaḥsaap* 'kill' and *ˀuukʷił* 'doing to' is the same. The semantic content of a single clause *qaḥsaap* 'kill' is 'spread over' multiple clauses *qaḥsaap* 'kill' and *ˀuukʷił* 'doing to' in order to split the salient participants into separate clauses.

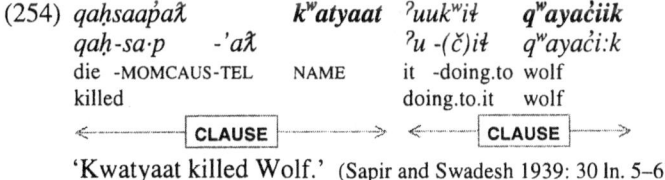

4.4.2.1.2. Meanings Expressed with Serialization

A complex predication can consist of clauses with a variety of meanings. The relative order between the two serialized clauses is flexible, or more precisely, sensitive to discourse needs: information that the speaker feels noteworthy is positioned first. Serialization of more than two clauses occurs, but it is uncommon for a predication to contain more than two clauses with objects. Within a complex predication, predication-level suffixes are generally attached to the first predicate.

4.4.2.1.2.1. Action[9] + Location

A complex predication can consist of one predicate expressing an action and another expressing the location where the action or event takes place.

(255)

łiqʷił	*hiił.*
łiqʷ-ʻił	*hi:ł*
sit -being.in.the.house	be.there.in.the.house
ACTION	LOCATION

'He was sitting there in the house.' [Kingfisher 70]

(256)

siikaa	*hitačinƛ*	*maaqtusiis.*
si:k -(y)a·	*hita -činƛ*	
saling -CONT	get.there -getting.into.a.bay	NAME
sailing	entered.a.bay	
ACTION	LOCATION	

'They sailed into the bay of Maaqtusiis.' [Kingfisher 2]

The relative order of predicates can vary.

(257)

hiłḥʔaƛ	*Friendship Center*	*mamuuk*	*Charlotte.*
hił -(q)ḥ -'aƛ		*mamu:k*	
be.there -SIM -TEL		work	
she.was.there		work	
LOCATION		ACTION	

'Charlotte was working at the Friendship Center.' [CLLS 275]

---

9 Predicates expressing an event and state typically behave similarly to action predicates, and thus they participate in a similar set of SERIALIZATION construction. Here I subsume them under 'action' predicates for the sake of convenience.

(258)

hiẏaaˀaƛquučˀał						*ˀiicˀiiqḥa.*
hił	*-'a·*	*-'aƛ*	*-qu:*	*-č*	*-ˀa·ł*	*ˀi:cˀi:qḥ-a·*
be.there	-being.on.the.rock	-TEL	-COND.3	-INF	-PL	tell.story -DUR
they.would.be.on.the.rocks						telling.stories
LOCATION						**ACTION**

'They would be on the rocks, telling stories to each other.' [Qawiqaalth 92]

4.4.2.1.2.2. Action + Time

A complex predication can consist of one predicate expressing an action and another expressing the time at which the action takes place.

(259)

sayaˀii	*ˀuušyuuya.*
saya -ˀi:	*ˀu:š -yu:ya*
far.off -reaching	some -being.at.the.time
went.far	sometimes
ACTION	**TEMPORAL**

'He sometimes went far.' [Mink 221]

(260)

ˀin	*čuuẏiiḥanit*				*ˀaˀum.*
ˀin	*ču*	*-ẏi·ḥa*	*-'at*	*-it*	*ˀaˀum*
though	have.an.odor	-suffering.excessive?	-SHIFT	-PAST	be.at.first
though	they.smelled.him				at.first
	ACTION				**TEMPORAL**

'although they smelled him at the beginning' [Qawiqaalth 101]

(261)

ˀaˀums	*wałaak*	*ˤaˀuknak*	*1919*
ˀaˀum -s	*wała:k*		
be.at.first -1sg	go	NAME	
I.first	went	Auknak	
TEMPORAL	**ACTION**		

'I first went to Auknak in 1919.' [GLLS 31]

(262)

qiičiˀaƛs				*suutił*	*ḥaaḥuupa*
qi:	*-či(ƛ)*	*-'aƛ*	*-s*	*sut -(č)ił*	*ḥa:ḥu:p -a·*
for.long	-MOM	-TEL	-1sg	you -doing.to	teach -DUR
I.have.been.doing.for.long				to.you	teaching
TEMPORAL					**ACTION**

'I have been teaching you [how to fish] for a long time.' [GLLS 117]

(263)

huuʔakʔaƛquus	*mamuuk.*
hu:ʔak-'aƛ -qu:s	*mamu:k*
early -TEL -COND.1sg	work
I.would.do.early	work
TEMPORAL	**ACTION**

'I used to work early in the morning.' [GLLS 147]

4.4.2.1.2.3. Action + Manner

A complex predication can consist of one predicate expressing an action and another expressing the manner in which the action or event is achieved or progresses.

(264)

wik̓at	*kaapap̓at*	*c̓aawačiƛʔat.*
wik-'at	*ka:pap -'at*	*c̓awa· -či(ƛ)-'at*
not -SHIFT	prefer - SHIFT	one -MOM - SHIFT
not	prefer	single.out
ACTION		**MANNER**

'Never show favoritism.'
'Never prefer one person.' [Qawiqaalth 24]

(265)

wiksłiiḥw̓iłas	*kamatquk*
wik-słi:ḥ -w̓iłas	*kamatq-uk*
not -taking.direction -about.to	run -DUR
without.taking.direction	be.running
MANNER	**ACTION**

'He was going to run frantically [without taking a specific direction].' [Mink 136]

(266)

č̓uḥiy̓ap	*łiʔuup*	*ʔuuštup*
č̓uḥ -iy̓ap	*łi -ʔu:p*	*ʔu:štup*
be.extinguished -MOMCAUS	throw -MOMCAUS	something
extinguish	throw	something
ACTION	**MANNER**	

'He extinguished the fire by throwing something.' [Wolf 11]

(267)

waasiḥ	*waaʔat*	*kaʔupšiʔat,*
wa:si-ḥ	*wa·-'at*	*kaʔup -ši(ƛ) -'at*
where -INTER.3	say -SHIFT	mention -MOM -SHIFT
where.is.he	they.asked	mentioned
	ACTION	**MANNER**

'"Where is he?", they asked them, mentioning his name.' [Kingfisher 154]

(268) *ḥaˀukˤiˀat,* *mačinƛ* *ƛaˀuukʷiˀatḥˀi.*
ḥaˀuk -ˤi(ƛ) -'at *mač -inƛ* *ƛaˀu:kʷiˀatḥ -ˀi·*
eat -coming.upon -SHIFT enter -MOM Clayoquot -DEF
they.caught.them.eating enter.house the.Clayoquot.man
ACTION **MANNER**
'The Clayoquot man came into the house when they were eating.' [Kingfisher 151]

(269) *č̓iiqaa* *ɬuucsamiiḥ* *y̓imy̓aaxa.*
č̓i:q -a· *ɬu:csami:ḥ* *y̓imy̓a:x -a·*
sing -DUR women chanting -DUR
sing women chanting
ACTION **MANNER**
'Women were chanting in middle-high voice.' [Wolf 15]

4.4.2.1.2.4. Action + Action

A complex predication can consist of one predicate expressing an action and another expressing an accompanying action or situation surrounding the first action.

(270) *qiiyuuk̓ʷaaɬ,* *hiščačiƛ* *ḥuuɬ,*
qi: -(y)u·k̓ʷa:ɬ *hiš -ca -či(ƛ)* *ḥu:ɬ*
be.for.long -being.absent be.all -going.to -MOM yonder
be.gone.long went.everywhere yonder
ACTION **ACTION**
'They were away for a long time, going everywhere.' [Qawiqaalth 105]

(271) *ˤiḥak* *ɬuucmaˀi* *hiniiˀas.*
ˤiḥ -ak *ɬu:cma -ˀi·* *hin -i:ˀas*
cry -DUR woman -DEF get.there -going.outside
crying the.woman go.out
ACTION **ACTION**
'The woman was crying as she came out.' [Kingfisher 40]

(272) *hinaačiƛˀaɬ,* *maakˀatu,* *k̓ʷak̓ʷaƛ,*
hin -a·či(ƛ) -ˀa·ɬ *mak -ˀatu* *k̓ʷak̓ʷaƛ*
get.there -going.out.to.meet -PL trad -falling.off sea.otter
they.go.out.to.meet trading sea.otter
ACTION **ACTION**
'They [native people] went to trade sea otters.' [Kingfisher 18]

4.4.2.1.2.5. Action + Relational

A complex predication can consist of one predicate expressing an action and another predicate that relates an entity or concept to the main action.[10] The predicate at the core of the clause serving the entity-relating function shares the same subject with the predicate expressing the main action and takes as its object the entity to be related to the main action. For example, in (141) the predicate in the relational clause *ʔuʔukʷink* 'doing together with' has the same subject as the predicate expressing the main action and has as its object the entity to be related to the main action, i.e., *kʷakuucuk* 'her grandchildren'.

(273)	*šišaa*	***ʔuuʔatup***	*kʷakuucuk,*
	šiš -(y)a·	*ʔu -'atup*	*kʷaku:c -uk*
	clean -CONT	it -doing.for	grandchild -POSS
	cleaning	doing.for	her.grandchildren
	ACTION	**RELATIONAL**	

'She would peel them for her grandchildren.' [CLLS 85]

Prototypical relational clauses are based on a transitive predicate that is semantically abstract, expressing only a general relational concept rather than a concrete action/event/state.

(274)	*wik*	*łačiƛ*	*David Frank*	***ʔuukʷił.***
	wik	*łač -i(ƛ)*		*ʔu -kʷił*
	not	let.go-MOM		it -doing.with.ref.to
	not	gave.up		with.ref.to.him
	ACTION			**RELATIONAL**

'He never left David Frank.' [CLLS 66]

(275)	*ʔimč̓aaq̓y̓ak*	***ʔuʔukʷink***	*kakaw̓in.*
	ʔimč̓a:q̓y̓ak	*ʔu -kʷink*	*kakaw̓in*
	play	it -being.together.with	killer.whale
	play	doing.together	killer.whale
	ACTION	**RELATIONAL**	

'He played with killer whales.' [Qawiqaalth 120]

(276)	*haaˤinčiʔaƛ̓atqʷin*	***ʔuḥʔat***	*Jacob Gallicit.*
	ha:ˤin -či(ƛ)-'aƛ̓ -'at -qʷin	*ʔuḥ -'at*	*Jacob Gallic-it*
	invite -MOM -TEL -SHIFT -COND.1pl	be.he -SHIFT	-PAST
	we.were.invited	being.by.him	late.Jacob.Gallic
	ACTION	**RELATIONAL**	

'We were invited by the late Jacob Gallic.' [CLLS 263]

[10] See Rose's (1981) discussion of 'NP-relating obliques'; Jacobsen's (1979a, 1993) of 'prepositional clauses'.

The entity-relating function can be most clearly discerned in relation to the serialized construction involving a transitive predicate that does not make a substantial semantic contribution. Compare the above examples with the following, where the serialized transitive predicate makes a more substantial semantic contribution. The entity-relating function of the serialized predicate becomes less distinct in comparison with the manner function discussed above.

(277)	*powersaw*	***ˀuuḥw̓aɬˀaƛ̓***	*čitšiˀat.*
		ˀu -ḥw̓aɬ -'aƛ̓	*čit -ši(ƛ̓)-'at*
		it -using -TEL	saw -MOM -SHIFT

'You use a powersaw to saw.' [Canoe 54]

(278)	*huˀinˀaqƛ̓*	***ˀuuktis***	*hupaɬˀi.*
	huˀa-in -ˀa·qƛ̓	*ˀu -ktis*	*hupaɬ -ˀi*
	back -coming -FUT	it -acting.by.ref.to	moon -DEF
	would.return	according.to	the.moon

'They would return according to the moon.' [Wolf 109]

However, the entity-relating function is not necessarily a property of predicates with abstract relational meanings. Predicates that express concrete actions/events/states can serve the entity-relating function. In the following examples, the predicates, *ˀuˀiič̓at* 'eating ...', *ˀuˀuˀiiḥ* 'gathering ...', and *ˀun̓aaḥ* 'seeking ...', seem to be used only to relate the entities expressed as objects to the state of affairs expressed by the other clauses, rather than to denote concrete actions.

(279)	*wikˀaatat*	*haˀukʷ̓at*	***ˀuˀiič̓at***	*hačˀinštup*
	wik-ˀa·ta -'at	*haˀuk -'at*	*ˀu -'i·c -'at*	*hačˀinštup*
	not -lacking -SHIFT	eat -SHIFT	it -consuming -SHIFT	food.from.deep.water
	we.never.lack	we.eat	eating.it	food.from.deep.water
	ACTION		**RELATIONAL**	

'We never lack food from low tide to eat.' [GLLS 54]

(280)	*ˀacyuuˀaƛ̓quuč*	***ˀuˀuˀiiḥ***	*ƛ̓iḥapiiḥ.*
	ˀac -yu· -'aƛ̓ -qu: -č	*ˀu -'i:ḥ*	*ƛ̓iḥapi:ḥ*
	go.out.fishing -done -TEL -COND.3 -INF	it -hunting	red.snapper
	would.be.out.for.food	hunting.it	red.snapper
	ACTION	**RELATIONAL**	

'He would go out fishing for red snapper.' [GLLS 68]

(281)	*ˀuuwaˀat*	***ˀun̓aaḥ***	*ƛułquu*
	ˀu -(w)a(ƛ)-'at	*ˀu -n̓a·ḥ*	*ƛuł -qu:*
	it -finding -SHIFT	it -seeking	good -COND.3
	one.finds	seek.it	good
	ACTION	**RELATIONAL**	
	'look for a good one' [Canoe 39]		

The entity-relating predicate is frequently based on the referential root *ˀu-*. This, however, is not a structural requirement for serialization of this type. Compare (282) with (283) and (284) below.

(282)	*humwic̓aƛatqʷin*	***ˀuuqḥłi***	*quˀišinm̓it.*
	humwic̓a -'aƛ -'at -qʷin	*ˀu -qḥłi*	*quˀišin -m̓i·t*
	tell.myth -TEL -SHIFT -COND.1pl	it -telling.about	raven -son.of
	she.would.tell.us.stories	tell.about.it	Son.of.Raven
	'She used to tell us stories about Son of Raven.' [CLLS 175]		

(283)	*huˀacačiƛ*	*načiqs*	***wałaak***
	huˀa-ca -či(ƛ)	*načiqs*	*wała:k*
	back -going.to -MOM	Tofino	go
	returned	Tofino	go
	'They went back to Tofino.' [Kingfisher 190]		

(284)	*yakquuˀa*	***n̓aacsa***	*qʷaaˀapˀitq.*
	yak -qu: -'a·	*n̓a:csa*	*qʷa: -'ap -ˀi·tq*
	watch -being.at.a.point -being.on.the.rock	see	thus -CAUS -REL.3
	watching.at.the.point	see	the.way.they.do
	'He was watching at the point what white men were doing.' [Kingfisher 163]		

The predicates *ˀuuqḥłi* 'tell about' in (282) and *wałaak* 'go' and *n̓aacsa* 'see' in (283) and (284) cannot be distinguished: none of them makes a significant semantic contribution beyond relating their objects to the main action/event predicate in rather general ways; the entities expressed by their objects are emphasized or contrasted with other entities. Thus, the entity-relating predicate does not have to be based on *ˀu-*. The frequent association of the referential root *ˀu-* with the entity-relating serialization most likely has to do with the fact that *ˀu-* is used to introduce an entity that is important in discourse.

In sum, the entity-relating function is associated with a construction where a transitive predicate does not make any substantial semantic contribution to the meaning of the complex predication. The class of predicates that can participate in this construction is open in that we cannot determine all the members. The variety of relationship expressed by the entity-relating predicate is also open.

The prototypical entity-relating clause (as illustrated in 274 through 276) has sometimes been called a 'prepositional clause' (Jacobsen 1979a, 1993). Although the term 'preposition' could be interpreted either as a specification of a lexical category or as a characterization of function, it is argued here that neither way could it be appropriate.

As a lexical category Nuuchahnulth does not have 'preposition'. As Jacobsen (1979a: 128) points out, predicates in 'prepositional clauses' are not sharply different from other transitive predicates in internal structure or external distribution. Thus, it is not possible in Nuuchahnulth to define a set of lexical items, whether at the morpheme level or at the word level, whose function is inherently limited to the 'prepositional' function. (See 3.1 for more discussion on lexical categories in Nuuchahnulth.)

As a functional characterization of a predicate the term 'prepositional' is misleading. First, it can lead to an incorrect view of the domain consisting of serialized clauses. The notion of 'preposition' typically presupposes a grammatically dependent relationship to the main predicate within a highly grammaticized structural domain comparable to a 'clause' in English. The presupposed structural features are, however, absent from entity-relating serialization in Nuuchahnulth: structural dependency cannot be established unequivocally, nor does the complex based on serialization, i.e., predication, form a highly grammaticized structural domain. (For more discussion, see section 4.3 on the nature of argument structure, and also see the section immediately below.) Thus, the characterization of the entity-relating predicate as a 'preposition' can lead to overstructuralization.

Second, the term 'prepositional' may suggest that the entity-relating serialization is a highly grammaticized construction in which the number of predicates that participate in the construction and also of the range of relations expressed by the construction is limited. As mentioned above, this is not the case.

Thus, it is best to avoid characterizing the entity-relating clause as a 'prepositional clause'. Rose's (1981) notion of 'NP-relating predicates' seems to be a better alternative in that it captures more accurately the fact that the entity-relating predicates represent a functional type rather than a structural class.

4.4.2.1.3. Structural Relationship between Serialized Clauses

Clauses combined through serialization are structurally on a par with each other: no structural dependency can be unequivocally established between serialized clauses. This lack of structural dependency between clauses frees the relative ordering of clauses to be exploited for discourse purposes.

The relative ordering of clauses depends on what aspect of the event is highlighted in discourse: the clause expressing the highlighted aspect of the event precedes the clause expressing the peripheral aspect of the event. Predication-level peripheral suffixes attach to the first predicate. Compare the pairs of examples in (285) through (287) below.

(285)

a.

wik	*łačiƛ*		*David Frank*	***ʔuukʷił.***
wik	*łač -i(ƛ)*			*ʔu -kʷił*
not	letting.go -MOM			it -being.with.ref.to
not	gave.up			with.ref.to.him
ACTION				**RELATIONAL**

'He never left David Frank.' [CLLS 66]

b.

ʔuukʷiłʔaƛna	*Bruce Kiblemit*	*ʕaačiƛ*
ʔu -(kʷ)ił -'aƛ -na·	*Bruce Kible-mit*	*ʕa:čiƛ*
it -being.with.ref.to -TEL -1pl	-PAST	ask.for.help
we.did.to.him	late.Bruce.Kible	ask.for.help
RELATIONAL		**ACTION**

'We asked the late Bruce Kible to help us.' [CLLS 231]

(286)

a.

ʔaaqičiłk	*huḥtakšiƛ*	***ʔaʔim,***
ʔaqi -čił -k	*huḥtak -ši(ƛ)*	*ʔaʔim*
what -being.with.ref.to -2sg	know -MOM	beginning
what.to.you	know	beginning
STATE		**TIME**

'What do you remember from the early days?' [CLLS 3]

b.

ʔaʔimyiis	*huḥtakšiƛ*	*ʔuuwaƛs*	*ʔin*	*ʔayaqƛasna.*
ʔaʔim -(y)i:s	*huḥtak -ši(ƛ)*	*ʔu -(w)aƛ -s*	*ʔin*	*ʔaya-'aqƛas -na·*
be.first -INDF.1sg	know -MOM	it -coming.upon -1sg	that	many-being.in.the.house-1pl
I.firstly	know	I.come.upon.it	that	many.of.us.in.the.house
TIME	**STATE**			

'My earliest memory is that I was in a household with many people.' [CLLS 4]

(287)

a.

ʔiinaxyaƛquuč	***ʔuušyuuya,***	*ʔiiḥ*	*ḥaw̓ił,*
ʔi:nax -yu· -'aƛ -qu: -č	*ʔu:š -yu:ya*	*ʔi:ḥʷ*	*ḥaw̓ił*
be.dressed.up -done -TEL -COND.3 -INF	some -being.at.the.time	great	leader
would.wear.uniform	sometimes	great	leader
ACTION	**TIME**		

'The respectable captain would sometimes wear the uniform.' [Kingfisher 34]

b.

ʔuušyuuyaƛquuč	*čamas,*	*teaʔii.*
ʔu:š -yu:ya -'aƛ -qu: -č	*čamas*	*tea -ʔi·*
some -being.at.the.time -TEL -COND.3 -INF	sweet	tea -DEF
sometimes.it.was	sweet	the.tea
TIME	**STATE**	

'Sometimes the tea was sweet.' [Kingfisher 206]

According to this view, the alternation between (a) and (b) in the above examples is a matter of the relative ordering of serialized clauses. This, however, is not necessarily self-evident or uncontroversial.

Such an alternation could be considered to involve a change in the hierarchical structure (see Rose 1981): for example, in (287a) *ˀuušyuuya* 'sometimes' would be structurally dependent on the main predicate *ˀiinaxyaƛ* 'be dressed up', while in (287b) *ˀuušyuuya* would be the main predicate. Thus, in the hierarchical view, the above alternation is not just a matter of ordering. The combined predicates are considered to be in a structural dependency relationship as opposed to a structurally equal relationship. This difference between the hierarchical view and the nonhierarchical view stems from the difference in how the two approaches consider the nature of predication-level suffixation. As noted above, in a complex predication only one predicate can carry predication-level suffixes, leaving other predicates without predication-level suffixes. The hierarchical view links the presence and absence of predication-level suffixes to 'finiteness' or grammatical completeness of a predicate: thus, a predicate with predication-level suffixes would be a grammatically complete, independent form, while a predicate without these suffixes would be a grammatically incomplete, dependent form.[11] In this view predication-level suffixes are considered to be a grammatical property of each predicate. The present approach, in contrast, considers predication-level suffixes to be a grammatical property of the whole predication. In other words, the presence and placement of predication-level suffixes are grammatically relevant only in relation to the predication as a whole. Therefore, the association of predication-level suffixes with a particular predicate within a complex predication is incidental. That is, predication-level suffixes are not inherently associated with a particular predicate, and the attachment pattern of predication-level suffixes, i.e., the first predicate in the predication, is systematic only at the predication level and appears arbitrary in relation to each predicate. Thus, in the present approach the presence and absence of predication-level suffixes is not linked to the structural completeness of a predicate. (See also the discussion on 'finiteness' in section 4.2.3.)

Although this difference between the two approaches may appear arbitrary, there are some considerations that make the present approach preferable. Consider again (286), repeated here as (288) for convenience.

[11] This view of the internal structure of a serialized complex is extended further when Jacobsen (1979a, 1993) characterizes certain entity-relating predicates without predication-level suffixes as 'prepositional clauses'.

(288)

a.

ˀaaqičiɬk			*huḥtakšiƛ*		***ˀaˀim**,*
ˀaqi	*-čiɬ*	*-k*	*huḥtak*	*-ši(ƛ)*	*ˀaˀim*
what	-being.with.ref.to	-2sg	know	-MOM	beginning
what.to.you			know		beginning
STATE					**TIME**

'What do you remember from the early days?' [CLLS 3]

b.

ˀaˀimyiis		*huḥtakšiƛ*		*ˀuuwaƛs*			*ˀin*	*ˀayaqƛ̓asna.*	
ˀaˀim	*-(y)i:s*	*huḥtak*	*-ši(ƛ)*	*ˀu*	*-(w)aƛ*	*-s*	*ˀin*	*ˀaya-'aqƛ̓as*	*-na·*
be.first	-INDF.1sg	know	-MOM	it	-coming.upon	-1sg	that	many-being.in.the.house-1pl	
I.firstly		know		I.come.upon.it			that	many.of.us.in.the.house	
TIME		**STATE**							

'My earliest memory is that I was in a household with many people.' [CLLS 4]

The alternation involves a change in the relative ordering of serialized clauses and also a change in the pattern of association between clauses and predication-level suffixes: in (288a) the clause expressing a temporal notion *ˀaˀim* 'at the beginning' occurs sentence-finally, whereas in (288b) *ˀaˀim* precedes the expression of a state. This alternation in the relative ordering coincides with the alternation in the presence/absence of predication-level suffixes: the sentence-initial clause carries predication-level suffixes but the noninitial clause does not. In the hierarchical approach, as just noted, the presence/absence of predication-level suffixes determines the syntactic characteristics of the clause, and therefore *ˀaˀim* in (288a) and (288b) is claimed to be syntactically different: one is a clausal adjunct and the other a main predicate (see Rose 1981: §3.3.2). Thus, there is no structural connection between (288a) and (288b) with reference to *ˀaˀim*. In other words, they are unrelated constructions that happen to be used to express pragmatic alternations. In the present approach, on the other hand, the presence/absence of predication-level suffixes is incidental at the clause level and therefore *ˀaˀim* has syntactically equal status in (288a) and (288b). The only difference is its relative position within the sentence. Thus, the alternation between (288a) and (288b) is one of word order, not of hierarchical structure. The distribution of predication-level suffixes is governed by a pattern beyond the level of the clause; predication-level suffixes are attached to the first predicate in the predication, regardless of the semantic or other characteristics of the predicate. This account of the alternation according to the present approach has two advantages. First, it is more systematic in that it characterizes the alternation as a phenomenon where syntactic and pragmatic structuring coincide rather than as a pragmatic association between structurally unrelated constructions. Second, it is a more general account in that it ascribes the alternation to a general trend in Nuuchahnulth syntax to use fronting as a strategy to highlight a certain element in discourse. (See section 4.7.1.2 for a discussion of argument ordering.)

4.4.2.1.4. Relative Ordering of Serialized Clauses

As discussed above, the relative order among serialized clauses is inherently flexible: that is, there is no inherent grammatical requirement that governs the order of serialized clauses. However, for some pairs of clauses, there are noticeable skewings in the ordering pattern in terms of textual frequency. When a clause expressing an action is serialized with one expressing a location, the two clauses tend to appear in the order ACTION–LOCATION (in 30 out of 44 cases or 68.2 percent). But when a clause expressing an action is serialized with one expressing a time, the order of the clauses is more likely be TIME–ACTION (in 37 out of 50 cases or 74 percent; Rose 1981: 62 reports a similar observation).

4.4.2.2. Modification

In MODIFICATION one predicate restricts the interpretation of the other semantically main predicate. Verbal modification is parallel to nominal modification in that the scope of a semantic contribution of the nonmain predicate is limited to the main predicate. Unlike nominal modification, however, the headedness phenomenon is not very meaningful in verbal modification. Because both predicates in verbal modification are verbal, the question of which predicate determines the syntactic behavior of the whole complex is not relevant.

As in nominal modification, suffixes are attached to the predicate that comes first, which is typically the modifying predicate. The following examples illustrate the placement of predication-level peripheral suffixes.

(289)

ˀiiḥˀaƛ̓atquus				*ˀuuˀaałuk̓ʷat*		
ˀi:ḥʷ	*-'aƛ̓*	*-'at*	***-qu:s***	*ˀu*	*-'a:łuk*	*-'at*
greatly	-TEL	-SHIFT	-COND.1sg	it	-looking.after	-SHIFT
they.did.to.me.a.lot				looking.after.me		
MODIFIER				**MODIFIED**		

'They looked after me very well.' [CLLS 14]

(290)

hiikʷałšiˀat			*k̓ʷačšiˀat.*		
hi:kʷał	*-ši(ƛ̓)*	***-ˀa·ł***	*k̓ʷač*	*-ši(ƛ̓)*	*-'at*
nearly	-MOM	-PL	hit.the.right.spot	-MOM	-SHIFT
they.almost.did			hit.the.right.place		
MODIFIER			**MODIFIED**		

'They almost made a direct hit at him.' [Wolf 132]

(291) ***ˀaanisa*** *ˁaċikšiƛ.*
ˀa:ni ***-sa*** *ˁaċik -ši(ƛ)*
really -1sg know.how.to -MOM
I.really learned.how.to
MODIFIER **MODIFIED**
'I really learned how to do it.' [CLLS 115]

In my current database, the modifying predicate predominantly precedes the modified predicate. However, it is not possible at this point to determine the definitive ordering pattern mainly because the number of instances of verbal modification is not large.

4.4.2.3. Complementation

COMPLEMENTATION is an expansion strategy of combining a predicate and a clause or a predication in a semantically hierarchical relationship where a clause or predication supplements the notion expressed by the main predicate. The main predicate and its complement are tied closely, and extraneous predicates do not occur between them. The relative ordering between the main predicate and its complement is fixed: the complement always follows the main predicate.

The expression serving as a complement could be characterized as 'syntactically dependent' in the sense that its syntactic position is fixed in relation to the main predicate. However, the complement is not 'dependent' in the formal sense that its form is in any way grammatically or distributionally defective.

Complementation can be found in several constructions: constructions based on 'complement-taking' predicates, negative expressions, and nonpolar questions.

4.4.2.3.1. Complement-Taking Predicates

Some predicates call for complementation. These predicates typically express abstract or higher-level concepts that are to be interpreted with reference to a concrete action, event, or state, much like 'complement-taking verbs' in English. In the following examples, predicative words expressing abstract concepts, *ˁaċik* 'be expert at' and *łiˀaaˀap* 'miss', need to be interpreted with reference to concrete actions, *tutušk̓iiḥ* 'fishing for cod' and *ƛičiƛ* 'shoot', respectively.

(292) ***ˤačikƛa*** ***tutuškiiḥ*** *qawiqaaɬ.*
ˤačik -ƛa· *tušk -'i:ḥ* *qawiqa:ɬ*
be.expert.at -again cod -hunting Qawiqaalth
also.expert.at fishing.for.cod Qawiqaalth
MAIN **COMPLEMENT**
'Qawiqaalth was also good at fishing for cod.' [Qawiqaalth 146]

(293) ***ɬiˀaaˀap̓at*** ***ƛičiˀat.***
ɬiˀa:-'ap -'at *ƛi -či(ƛ)-'at*
miss -CAUS -SHIFT shoot -MOM -SHIFT
they.missed.him they.shot.him
MAIN **COMPLEMENT**
'They [the British] missed their shot at him.' [Kingfisher 151]

4.4.2.3.1.1. Clauses as Complements

The expression serving as a complement can take a variety of shapes. It can be a clause, as in the following examples. In many cases the subject of the main predicate and that of the complement predicate are coreferential, as shown in examples (294) through (298).

(294) *ˀuˀumḥimataks* ***kʷixsaqsiƛ***
ˀuˀumḥi -matak -s *kʷis -<x> -aqs -iƛ*
be.able.to -probably -1sg be.different -MINK -being.on.the.side -MOM
maybe.I.can.do reach.the.opposite.shore
MAIN **COMPLEMENT**
'Maybe I can go across the strait.' [Mink 13]

(295) *ḥaaˀuqḥšiiɬˀaɬ,* ***kutḥy̓akʷaqƛn̓uk*** ***nunuuk.***
ḥaˀu -(q)ḥ -ši:ɬ -ˀa·ɬ *kutḥ -y̓akʷ -'aqƛ -n̓uk* *nunu:k*
do.in.turn -SIM -ITER -PL drum -device -being.inside? -being.in.hand singing
they.kept.taking.turns holding.a.drum.in.the.hand singing
MAIN **COMPLEMENT**
'They would take turns drumming and singing.' [CLLS 273]

(296) *kuw̓iɬas* ***ƛiˤiiƛ.***
kuw̓iɬa -s *ƛiqʷ-'i·(ƛ)*
obey -1sg sit -getting.on.the.ground
I.obey sit.down
MAIN **COMPLEMENT**
'I sat as I was told.' [CLLS 113]

(297)

ˀaḥˀaaƛ	*ˀunic*	*hawiiˀaƛ*	***dog salmon***	***ˀuˀuˀiiḥ***
ˀaḥˀa:-'aƛ	*ˀunic*	*hawi:(ƛ) -'aƛ*		*ˀu -'i:ḥ*
then -TEL	time.elapsed	finish -TEL		it -hunting
then	in.a.little.while	finished		hunting.it
		MAIN	**COMPLEMENT**	

'Then after a while the season for dog salmon ended.' [GLLS 120]

(298)

nasaƛna	***ḥačxʷinƛˀaqƛ.***
nas -'aƛ -na·	*ḥačxʷinƛ -ˀa·qƛ*
try.in.vain -TEL -1pl	go.deeper -FUT
we.failed	will.go.deeper
MAIN	**COMPLEMENT**

'We could not go deep.' [Qawiqaalth 88]

The subject of the complement predicate can be different from that of the main predicate.

(299)

k̓ʷaččiˀaƛƛa	***muułšiƛ,***
k̓ʷač -ši(ƛ)-'aƛ -ƛa·	*mu:ł -ši(ƛ)*
hit.the.right.spot -MOM -TEL -again	tide.is.up -MOM
went.just.in.time.again	the.tide.gets.high
MAIN	**COMPLEMENT**

'He got there just in time for the high tide.' [Kingfisher 176]

There are some impersonal predicates that take as a complement a predicate departicularized with the PERSPECTIVE-SHIFT suffix *-'at.* (For a detailed discussion of the DEPARTICULARIZING use of the PERSPECTIVE-SHIFT suffix *-'at* see 4.5.3.1.3.)

(300)

ˀuuščałit	***ciiqciiqat***
ˀu:ščał -it	*REDUP- ciq -a* ***-'at***
prohibited -PAST	ITER- speak -REP -SHIFT
it.was.prohibited	speaking
MAIN	**COMPLEMENT**

'We weren't allowed to talk [in our native language].' [GLLS 44]

(301)

ˀucuk	***nanaˀat,***
ˀu -cuk	*DUP- naˀa·* ***-'at***
it -needing	DISTR- understand -SHIFT
it.is.necessary	be.educated
MAIN	**COMPLEMENT**

'It is necessary to be educated.' [GLLS 148]

Predicates expressing a desire or intention can take a complement predicate with a different subject by taking the CAUSATIVE suffix. In (302), the main predicate of intention *č̓iṅuqƛ* 'unwilling to' and its complement predicate *wałšiƛ* 'go home' have different subjects, *they* and *I* respectively, and the main predicate is affixed with the CAUSATIVE -*'ap*.

(302) *ʔuy̓iiḥaƛatsa*	*č̓iňuqƛap̓atʔaɬ*	*waɬšiƛ*
ʔu -y̓i·ḥa -'aƛ -'at -sa	*č̓iňuqƛ* ***-'ap*** *-'at -ʔa·ɬ*	*waɬ -ši(ƛ)*
it -being.because.of -TEL -SHIFT -1sg	unwilling -CAUS -SHIFT -PL	go.home -MOM
because.of.it.they	they.were.unwilling.to.let	go.home
	MAIN	**COMPLEMENT**

'They [the priests and the nuns in charge] didn't want to let me go.' [CLLS 305]

In (303), the main predicate of desire *wik-maḥsa* 'not wanting' and its complement predicate *pawaɬšiƛ* 'get lost' have different subjects, *they* and *name* respectively, and the main predicate is affixed with the CAUSATIVE -*'ap*.

(303) *wikmaḥsap*	*pawaɬšiƛ*	*ʕimtii.*
wik -maḥsa ***-'ap***	*pawaɬ -ši(ƛ)*	*ʕimti:*
not -desiring.to -CAUS	lost -MOM	name
so.it.wouldn't	get.lost	name
MAIN	**COMPLEMENT**	

'[They do that] so that their name [title] will not be lost.' [Wolf 194]

4.4.2.3.1.2. Predications as complements

The complement can be a predication.[12] In this case, the complement represents a state of affairs separate from that of the main predication.

The complement predication can be associated directly with the main predicate without any overt formal indication of the hierarchical relationship. As in other types of complementation, the complement predication always follows the main predicate. For example, in (304) the complement expression *čiiqaa ḥaaw̓iɬaƛʔi* 'the young man was chanting' involves a separate set of participants and therefore constitutes an event that is separate from that expressed in the main predication.

(304) *naʔaaʔaƛquuč*	*mač̓ɬaatʔatḥ*	***čiiqaa***	***ḥaaw̓iɬaƛʔi.***
naʔa: -'aƛ -qu: -č		*či:q -(y)a·*	*ḥa:w̓iɬaƛ -ʔi·*
hear -TEL -COND.3 -INF	NAME	chant -CONT	young.man -DEF
they.would.hear.him	Muchalat	chant	the.young.man
MAIN		**COMPLEMENT**	

'Muchalat people would hear the young man chanting his song.' [Wolf 56]

[12] See the constructions labeled 'complement obliques' in Rose (1981: §3.2.5).

Similarly in (305) the expressions *ˀuuwaˀaƛatqʷin* 'if they catch us doing' and *ṅiƛaakna* 'we are fighting' constitute separate predications, as evidenced by the fact that both predicates carry a predication-level person suffix. (Note that the person suffix is fused with a mood suffix in the first predicate: see sections 2.4.3.1 and 2.4.3.2 for descriptions of forms of person and mood suffixes.)

(305) *ˀuuwaˀaƛatqʷin* **_ṅiƛaakna,_**
ˀu -(w)a(ƛ) -'aƛ -'at ***-qʷin*** *ṅiƛa:k-****na·***
it -coming.upon -TEL -SHIFT -COND.1pl fight -1pl
if.they.find.us.doing we.are.fighting
MAIN **COMPLEMENT**
'if they catch us fighting' [CLLS 181]

When the complement predication is counterfactual or otherwise irrealis, it is marked with the CONDITIONAL mood suffix, as in examples (306) through (310).

(306) *ˀaaḥˀasa* ***ˁuy̓inakquu.***
ˀa:ḥˀasa *ˁuy̓i -na·k* ***-qu:***
it.seems medicine -having -COND.3
it.seems as.if.they.had.medicine
MAIN **COMPLEMENT**
'It seems as though they had medicine.' [Wolf 165]

(307) *ˀuupap̓aƛquuč* *qawiqaał,* ***ḥačxʷiiqčikquu.***
ˀu -pap -'aƛ -qu: -č *qawiqa:ł* *ḥačxʷi· -qčik* ***-qu:***
it -preferring -TEL -COND.3 -INF Qawiqaalth deep.down -going.along -COND.3
would.prefer.it Qawiqaalth would.go.deeper
MAIN **COMPLEMENT**
'Qawiqaalth used to like to go deeper.' [Qawiqaalth 115]

(308) *wiksiiš* *huḥtak,*
wik-si·š *huḥtak*
not -IND.1sg know
I.do.not know
MAIN

ˀuušyuuyamitquus ***ṅiƛaak***
ˀu:š -yu:ya -mit ***-qu:s*** *ṅiƛa:k*
some -being.at.the.time -PAST -COND.1sg fight
I.would.have.done.sometimes fight
COMPLEMENT

yaqukʷitiis ***brother.***
yaq-ukʷ -it -(y)i:s
who-POSS -PAST -INDF.1sg
who.was.my

'I don't remember ever quarreling with my late younger brother.' [CLLS 190]

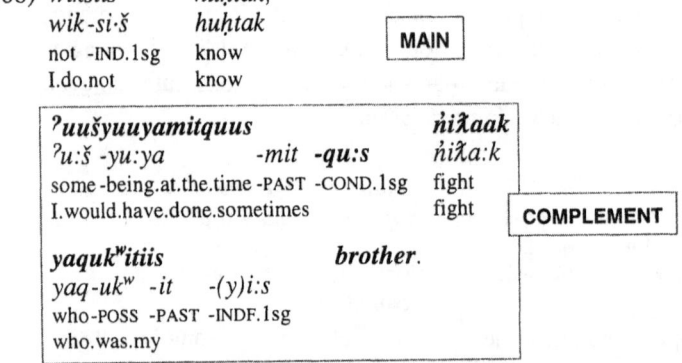

(309)	*wik*	*ˀuucḥa,*	***saaxyapanačšiƛˀaqƛquu.***	
	wik	*ˀu -cḥa*	*saya -<x>-panač*	*-ši(ƛ)-ˀaqƛ-**qu:***
	not	it -go.in.order.to	far.off -MINK -moving.about.randomly	-MOM -FUT -COND.3
	not	go.for.it	he.would.go.distant.places	
	MAIN		**COMPLEMENT**	

'[He went across the strait] not for the purpose of going to far-off places.' [Mink 15]

(310)	*ˀinisˀaaḥ*	***tiičquus***	***siy̓a.***
	ˀinis-'a:ḥ	*ti:č **-qu:s***	*siy̓a*
	wish -presumably	live -COND.1sg	I
	presumably.they.were.wishing	I.would.live	I
	MAIN	**COMPLEMENT**	

'Presumably [they prayed] wishing that I might live.' [CLLS 322]

4.4.2.3.2. Negation

A negative predication can consist of a single clause, as in examples (311) through (313), but it can also take an expanded form involving complementation, as in examples (314) and (315).

NEGATIVE PREDICATIONS BASED ON A SINGLE CLAUSE

(311) *wiikmaɬ,*
wik-maɬ
not -surviving

'There was none left.'
'None survived.' [Mink 264]

(312) *wikiɬ.*
wik-'iɬ
not -being.in.the.house

'He was gone.'
'He was not at home.' [Qawiqaalth 35]

(313) *wikiimits,*
wik-i:p -it -s
not -obtaining -PAST -1sg

'I didn't catch anything.' [Mink 297]

NEGATIVE PREDICATIONS INVOLVING COMPLEMENTATION

(314) *wik waʔičuƛ.*
wik waʔič-uƛ
not sleep -MOM
'He did not take any sleep.' [Mink 176]

(315) *wik̓aƛ haʔukšiƛ,*
wik-'aƛ haʔuk -ši(ƛ)
not -TEL eat -MOM
'He did not eat.' [Mink 266]

Expanded negative predications consist of a predicate expressing negativity and a complement clause expressing the state or event to be negated. Thus, in (314), the first predicate *wik* 'not' expresses negativity and the complement *waʔičuƛ* 'sleep' expresses the action to be negated. The relative order between the negative predicate and its complement is fixed: the former always precedes the latter. The following are additional examples.

(316) Negation of a property concept
wikckʷii ʔiiḥ.
wik-ckʷi· ʔi:ḥʷ
not -done be.large
'It was not big.' [Kingfisher 8]

(317) Negation of a state
a. ***wik tuuḥuk,***
wik tu:ḥuk
not afraid
'He was not scared.' [Mink 85]

b. ***wik̓aƛquuʔał č̓awiista***
wik-'aƛ -qu: -ʔa·ł č̓awa· -ista
not -TEL -COND.3 -PL one -having.persons.in.canoe
they.would.never.do alone.in.canoe
'They would never go out [on a canoe] alone.' [CLLS 74]

(318) Negation of a location
wik̓aƛquus hił, *qaaqaawis.*
wik-'aƛ -qu:s hił
not -TEL -COND.1sg be.there NAME
when.I.didn't be.there
'when I was not at Qaaqaawis' [CLLS 297]

(319) Negation of a qualifier

wik ˀaanaḥi, *watqšiˀat,*
wik ˀana-ḥi· *watq -ši(ƛ)-'at*
not only -DUR swallow -MOM -SHIFT

'You don't just swallow.' [CLLS 329]

(320) Negation of a manner

wik čamiḥta *haˀuk,*
wik čamiḥta haˀuk
not be.proper eat

'He does not eat properly.' [Mink 70]

(321) Negation of a quantifier

wik hišuk *y̓aaqn̓aq.*
wik hiš -uk y̓a:qn̓aq
not be.all-DUR be.long-winded

'Not all of them were long-winded.' [Kingfisher 149]

(322) Negation of a time

a. ***wikqiiḥsn̓aak***
wik qi: -ḥsn̓a·k
not be.for.long -being.in.between
not once.in.a.long.while

'It happened before long.' [Mink 81]

b. ***wik nay̓iik*** *mačinƛ.*
wik nay̓i:k mač -inƛ
not be.immediately enter -MOM

'He didn't enter the house right away.' [Dog 65]

(323) Negation of an event

wikiičiƛ ḥisaa.
wik-'i·či(ƛ) ḥis -(y)a·
not -INC blood -CONT
it.stopped bleeding

wik xʷakšiƛ.
wik xʷak -ši(ƛ)
not swollen -MOM
not get.swollen

'[Then] it [= his wound] stopped bleeding, and it didn't even swell.' [Wolf 166]

Other negative roots such as *wiiy̓a* 'never' are used in the same way as *wik* 'not':

(324) *wiiy̓a humaqƛ̓ic.*
wi:y̓a *humaqƛ̓ -'i·c*
never whole -consuming
never eat.the.whole
'He never eats the whole thing.' [Mink 116]

(325) *wiiy̓imtwaʔiš* *wiiqḥap*
wi:y̓a-*imt -wa·ʔi·š* *wi:q -ḥap*
never -PAST -QUOT.3 unpleasant -doing?
never.did do.harm

maaṅuuʔisʔatḥ qʷayac̓iik.
ma:ṅu:ʔisʔatḥ qʷayac̓i:k
Manhousat wolf
Manhousat wolf
'Manhousat people never did harm to wolves.' [Wolf 200]

4.4.2.3.3. Nonpolar Questions

Nonpolar questions in Nuuchahnulth take the form that can be considered a type of complementation, with the predicate expressing an interrogative notion serving as the main predicate and a complement clause expressing the event or state with respect to which the question is asked. For example, in (326) below, *ʔačaʕantk* 'who did … to you' expresses the interrogative notion and *quʔiiy̓ap̓at* 'raised' expresses the action with respect to which the question is asked.

(326) *ʔačaʕantk* *quʔiiy̓ap̓t*
ʔačaq-'at -it -k *qu -'i·y̓a·p -'at*
who -SHIFT -PAST -2sg person -INC.CAUS -SHIFT
who.did.it.to.you raised
'Who raised you?' [CLLS 12]

As in the typical complement construction, the relative order between the interrogative predicate and the action predicate is fixed. The following are additional examples:

(327)

ʔaaqičiłk		*huḥtakšiƛ*	*ʔaʔim,*
ʔaqi -čił	*-k*	*huḥtak -ši(ƛ)*	*ʔaʔim*
what -being.with.ref.to	-2sg	know -MOM	be.first
what.do.you.do		know	beginning

'What is the first thing you remember?' [CLLS 3]

(328)

ʔaqisḥw̓iłasʔaƛitḥ					*suw̓a*	*ʕinm̓iičiƛ.*
ʔaqisḥ	*-w̓iłas*	*-'aƛ*	*-it*	*-ḥ*	*suw̓a*	*ʕinm̓i-'i·či(ƛ)*
why	-about.to	-TEL	-PAST	-INTER.3	you	snail -INC
why.were.you.going.to.be					you	become.a.snail

'Why would you become a snail?' [CLLS 180]

(329)

ʔaqisḥitḥsuu			*šiiƛuk,*
ʔaqisḥ	*-it*	*-ḥsu:*	*ši:ƛuk*
why	-PAST	-INTER.2p	move
why.did.you			move

'Why did you move?' [CLLS 217]

4.5. The Manipulation of Participant Structure

Argument structure can be affected through the use of derivational morphemes, including *-'ap* CAUSATIVE, *-a·k* ~ *-uk* POSSESSIVE, and *-'at* PERSPECTIVE-SHIFT.

4.5.1. Causatives

The CAUSATIVE suffix ***-'ap*** affects the participant-taking characteristics of the predicate by introducing an instigator.[13] Grammatically the instigator is expressed as a subject.

(330) *haʔuk* 'he eats'
→ *haʔuk̓aps* [*haʔuk* + *-'ap* + *-s* 1sg]
'I make him eat.'
'I serve him a meal.'

---

[13] When the CAUSATIVE is added to a stem that ends in the MOMENTANEOUS aspect suffix, the MOMENTANEOUS aspect and CAUSATIVE are expressed by a syncretic suffix. The syncretic MOMENTANEOUS CAUSATIVE suffix takes different shapes depending on the shape of the momentaneous aspect suffix associated with the root: e.g., *-šiƛ* MOM → *-sa·p* MOMCAUS as in *qaḥsaap* 'kill' (cf. *qaḥšiƛ* 'die') and *haptsaap* 'hide ...' (cf. *haptšiƛ* 'be in hiding'); *-uƛ* MOM → *-u·p* MOMCAUS as in *m̓učičup* 'clothe someone' (cf. *m̓učičuƛ* 'get clothed') and *waʔičup* 'put someone to sleep' (cf. *waʔičuƛ* 'sleep').

(331) *huḥtakšiiḥ* 'they keep learning'
→ *huḥtakšiiḥaps* [*huḥtakšiiḥ* + -*'ap* + -*s* 1sg]
'I make them keep learning.'
'I keep teaching them.'

When structurally apparent, the agent of the caused action is grammatically coded as the object. In the following example, the agent of the caused action *tiič* 'live' is the first-person singular, and the IMPERATIVE mood suffix -*'i·s* denotes an action by the second-person singular on the first-person singular.

(332) *tiič̓ap̓is,*
ti:č **-'ap** -*'i·s*
be.alive-CAUS -IMP.2s>1s
keep.me.alive

'Let me live.' [Mink 260]

The following are additional examples of the causative construction:

(333) on an intransitive state
tačkʷaʔap *kuunaaqčisʔi.*
tačkʷa **-'ap** *ku:na:* -*qčis* -*ʔi·*
annihilated -CAUS schooner -people.on.board -DEF
annihilate the.people.on.the.schooner

'They [Ahousahts] killed all the people on the schooner.' [Kingfisher 66]

(334) on an intransitive action
k̓aḥkʷaʔap̓atuk *ƛ̓aḥiqs* *qʷinaakitiiʔał,*
k̓aḥ -*kʷa* **-'ap** -*'at* -*uk* *ƛ̓aḥ* -*iqs* *qʷi* -*na·k* -*it* -*(y)i:* -*ʔa·ł*
split -being.dispersed -CAUS -SHIFT -POSS flatwise -box what -having -PAST -INDF.3 -PL
broke.into.pieces box whatever.they.own

'They broke into pieces all the boxes.' [Kingfisher 161]

(335) on an intransitive event
ʕumaaʔap, *ʕuy̓aakʔi,*
ʕuma: **-'ap** *ʕuy̓i* -*ʔa·k* -*ʔi·*
running.water -CAUS medicine -POSS -DEF
let.water.run his.medicine.oil

'He poured out his medicine oil.' [Mink 182]

(336) on a location
hiɬˀapˀat ˀaḥ ˀappiˀiɬˀi.
hiɬ ***-'ap*** *-'at ˀaḥ ˀap -pi -'iɬ -ˀi·*
be.there -CAUS -SHIFT here LOC -being.in.the.middle -being.in.the.house -DEF
they.put.him.there here the.center.of.the.house

'They put him at the center.' [Wolf 77]

(337) on a location
ˀuˀiiˀasˀap k̓anisˀi čumˀiɬukʷiˀaɬ.
ˀu -ˀi: -'as ***-'ap*** *k̓anis -ˀi· čumˀiɬ -uk -i -ˀa·ɬ*
it -reaching -being.on.the.platform -CAUS stop.over -DEF bed -POSS-??-PL
put.him.on.the.platform one.who.stays.over their.bed

'They put people who stayed over on their beds.'
'They let people who stayed over use the beds.' [CLLS 51]

(338) on a transitive action
hupkčuu ˀuˀiič̓ap.
hupkču: ˀu -'i·c ***-'ap***
dumpling it -consuming -CAUS
dumpling serve.it

'They served them dumplings.' [JG.II 70]

(339) on a transitive state
numaak,
numa:k
forbidden
forbidden

ˀuḥtinˀap̓at č̓apac ˀuẃasckʷiˀi.
ˀu -ḥtin -'ap *-'at č̓apac ˀuxʷ -'as -ckʷi· -ˀi·*
it -being.made.of -CAUS -SHIFT canoe toppled.over -being.on.the.ground -happened -DEF
make.of.it canoe the.fallen.tree

'It is forbidden to make a canoe out of a windfall.' [Canoe 210]

(340) on a transitive action
ˀucaḥtaˀap̓at, čimˀiɬukʷitˀi,
ˀu -ca -ḥta ***-'ap*** *-'at čimˀiɬ -ukʷ -it -ˀi·*
it -going.to -being.headed.for -CAUS -SHIFT bed -POSS-PAST -DEF
they.brought.him his.bed

'They brought him to his bed.' [Dog 68]

The causative suffix *-'ap* can be attached to predicates that express meanings other than events or states. The following is an example involving entities.

(341) *ˀiiḥcamisˀap.*
*ˀi:ḥʷ-camis-**'ap***
great -thing -CAUS

'They celebrate it greatly.' [Kingfisher 227]

(342) *ˀuuškckʷaap̓atƛ̓a* *qʷisˀap̓at*
ˀu:š -ckʷi· ***-'ap*** *-'at -ƛ̓a·* *qʷis -'ap -'at*
some -remains.of -CAUS -SHIFT -again do.so -CAUS -SHIFT
some.also.have.been.left.before being.done.so

'There were some that survived [the killing] in the same way before.' [Mink 265]

When *-'ap* is associated with an entity, the resulting word expresses an action that brings about the entity as a result.

When *-'ap* is associated with a stem expressing manner or time, the resulting word expresses an action that is carried out in a specified manner or in a specified time frame, as shown in (343)–(346) and (347), respectively:

MANNER

(343) *ˀaḥ* *qʷaaˀap̓at.*
ˀaḥ *qʷa: **-'ap*** *-'at*
this thus -CAUS -SHIFT
this how.it.is.done

'This is how you do it.' [Canoe 47]

(344) *ḥamałap* *hiišił.*
*ḥamat **-'ap*** *hiš -ił*
plain -CAUS all -doing.with.ref.to
see.clearly as.for.all

'He could clearly see everything.' [Mink 10]

(345) *sačicaˀamitˀišˀał* *wałˁiiqƛ̓.*
*sačica **-'ap*** *-it -ˀi·š -ˀa·ł* *wałˁi:qƛ̓*
unceasingly? -CAUS -PAST -IND.3 -PL homesick
they.constantly.did homesick

'They constantly got homesick.' [CLLS 225]

(346) *ƛ̓uułḥap̓at.*
*ƛ̓u:ł -(q)ḥ **-'ap*** *-'at*
gentle -SIM -CAUS -SHIFT

'Do it slowly.' [CLLS 120]

TIME

(347)

wik̓at	*qiiˀap̓at.*		
wik-'at	*qi:*	***-'ap***	*-'at*
not -SHIFT	be.for.long	-CAUS	-SHIFT
don't	do.it.for.a.long.time		

'Don't do it for a long time.' [Canoe 230]

When the causative suffix *-'ap* is associated with a predicate that denotes desire or control, the resulting word does not necessarily express a direct causative event. Rather, it is interpreted that the person is wishing or doing something so that an event that is not under his direct control will occur.

(348)

čačimḥimaḥsap,			
čačim	*-ḥi·*	***-maḥsa***	***-'ap***
be.proper	-DUR	-wanting.to	-CAUS
want.to.make.proper			

'He wants to make it proper.' [Canoe 96]

(349)

hiniiˀasmaḥsaps				
hin	*-i·ˀas*	***-maḥsa***	***-'ap***	*-s*
get.there	-being.outside	-wanting.to	-CAUS	-1sg

'I want him out.' [elicited 94.7.7-37]

(350)

huˀacaay̓up		*wiiksinḥap̓at*			
huˀa-ca	*-y̓up*	*wik*	***-sinḥi***	***-'ap***	*-'at*
back -going	-MOMCAUS	not	-keeping.in.condition.of	-CAUS	-SHIFT
made.go.back		trying.to.prevent.from			

n̓aacsiičiƛ		*qʷiiwaƛii.*		
n̓a:csa	*-'i·či(ƛ)*	*qʷi*	*-(w)aƛ*	*-(y)i:*
see	-INC	that.which-find		-INDF.3
seeing		thing.that.we.found		

'He made me go back, trying to prevent me from seeing what we came across.' [Littles.I 81]

(351)

ˀuy̓iiḥaƛatsa					*čin̓uqƛap̓atˀał*				*wałšiƛ*	
ˀu	*-y̓i·ḥa*	*-'aƛ*	*-'at*	*-sa*	***čin̓uqƛ***	***-'ap***	*-'at*	*-ˀa·ł*	*wał*	*-ši(ƛ)*
it	-being.because.of	-TEL	-SHIFT	-1sg	unwilling	-CAUS	-SHIFT	-PL	go.home	-MOM
because.of.it.they					they.were.unwilling				go.home	

'Because of it, they didn't want me to go home.' [CLLS 305]

4.5.2. Possession

In Nuuchahnulth when an argument, either subject or object, is possessed, possession can be marked morphologically either on the argument or on the predicate. When it is expressed on the argument, the POSSESSIVE suffix is attached to the possessed along with a suffix indicating the person of the possessor. (The first- and second-person possessor forms also contain an additional mood suffix: SUBORDINATE mood for first person and RELATIVE mood for second person.)

(352) *ˀaapḥiiˀiš* *ɬuucmaakqs*
ˀa:p -ḥi· -ˀi·š *ɬu:cma -**ˀa·k -qs***
kind -DUR -IND.3 wife -POSS -SUB.1sg
'My wife is kind.' [elicited 7.19.94-53]

When possession is expressed on the predicate, the possessive suffix is attached to the predicate, and the possessor is indicated by the subject pronominal suffix. Thus, the argument structure, as indicated by morphology, is affected in such a way that the possessor becomes the subject.

(353) *ˀaapḥiiˀaks* *ɬuucma*
*ˀa:p -ḥi· -**ˀa·k -s*** *ɬu:cma*
kind -DUR -POSS -1sg wife
'My wife is kind.' [elicited 7.19.94-52]

The change in argument structure in the possessive-marked predicate is not limited to morphology: it is also reflected in the form of the independent pronoun and in the way the possessed argument interacts with the animacy hierarchy constraints. First, when there is an independent pronoun coreferential with the possessor, it is in the subject form, rather than the possessive form.

(354) *y̓ap̓icukkʷiis* ***siy̓aaq*** / ****siy̓aas***
y̓ap̓ic-uk ***-uk*** *-(y)i:s* *siy̓a:q* / **siy̓a:s*
blue -DUR -POSS-INDF.1sg I / mine
'Mine is blue!' [Rose 1981: 238][14]

Second, animacy hierarchy constraints operate as if the possessor, rather than the possessed, is the argument. In Nuuchahnulth transitive predications, certain participant relationships cannot be expressed directly: specifically, it is not permitted for a participant low in animacy to act on one high in animacy. Thus, a third person cannot act

---

[14] Although this example is from the Kyuquot dialect, the dialectal differences do not affect the validity of the example in this context.

on a speech-act participant (first or second), nor can a nontopical third person act on a topical third person. In order to express the prohibited participant relationships, the argument structure must be changed using the PERSPECTIVE-SHIFTING construction so that the high-animacy UNDERGOER[15] is the subject. (See the section 4.5.3 for a more detailed discussion of the animacy hierarchy constraints and the PERSPECTIVE-SHIFTING construction.) Interestingly, when a participant is possessed, the animacy constraint interacts with the animacy value of the possessor, not the possessed. In example (355) the third-person undergoer *hiyiqtup* 'things' is possessed by the first-person plural. The relationship between the actor (third person) and the possessed (third person) would not trigger the PERSPECTIVE-SHIFTING construction, whereas the relationship between the actor (third person) and the possessor (first person) would. The actual sentence is in the PERSPECTIVE-SHIFTING construction.

(355)	*m̓aw̓aaˀaƛatukʷina*					*hiyiqtup.*	
	m̓aw̓a:	*-'aƛ*	***-'at***	***-uk***	***-ina***	*hiyiq*	*-tu·p*
	deliver	-TEL	-SHIFT	-POSS	-1pl	various	-thing
	he.brought.our					things	

'He brought our things.' [CLLS 236]

What is relevant for the animacy hierarchy constraints is the animacy value of the possessor of the undergoer, rather than the possessed, the undergoer itself.

To recapitulate the above observations, in the construction where possession is marked on the predicate, (i) the possessor controls the subject pronominal suffix, (ii) the possessor is referred to by the subject form of the independent pronoun, (iii) the possessor interacts with the animacy hierarchy constraints. Based on these three observations, it seems safe to say that the possessor is behaving grammatically just like a true argument.

Thus, the two strategies of marking possession of a participant are in essence different choices of which grammatical argument participates in syntactic patterning: the possessed is chosen as a grammatical argument when possession is marked on the argument, and the possessor when possession marking is on the predicate.

The following are additional examples of possession marked on the predicate. Examples (356) and (357) illustrate cases involving possessed actors, whereas (358) and (359) illustrate cases with possessive undergoers.

---

[15] I use the terms ACTOR for participant with higher agency and UNDERGOER for that with lower agency. In a typical transitive predication the ACTOR is expressed as the subject and the UNDERGOER as the object. See footnote 17 for additional discussion of the terms.

EXAMPLES WITH POSSESSED ACTORS

(356)	*histaqšiƛukʷicuuš*					*ˤimtii*
	his	*-taq*	*-ši(ƛ)*	***-uk***	***-**ˀicu:š*	*ˤimti:*
	get.there	-coming.from	-MOM	-POSS	-IND.2pl	name
	yours.come.from.there					name

'Your name is from that region.' [JG.II 18]

(357)	*ˀuyaasiɬatuk*				*muunaa*	*Bruce.*
	ˀuya:	*-siɬa*	*-'at*	***-uk***	*mu·na·*	
	be.unusual	-acting.like	-SHIFT	-POSS	engine	
	something.went.wrong.with.his				engine	

'Bruce's engine stopped working.' [CLLS 233]

EXAMPLES WITH POSSESSED UNDERGOERS

(358)	*ˀin*	*m̓aw̓aaˀaƛatukʷina*					*hiyiqtup.*	
	ˀin	*m̓aw̓a:*	*-'aƛ*	*-'at*	***-uk***	*-ina*	*hiyiq*	*-tu·p*
	because	deliver	-TEL	-SHIFT	-POSS	-1pl	various	-thing
	because	delivered.our					everything	

'Because [later] he brought the rest of our things.' [CLLS 237]

(359)	*čiiˀatap̓atuks*						*čičiči*	*taaktaˀi.*	
	či:	*-ˀatu*	*-'ap*	*-'at*	***-uk***	*-s*	*čičiči*	*ta·kta*	*-ˀi·*
	pull	-falling.off	-CAUS	-SHIFT	-POSS	-1sg	teeth	doctor	-DEF
	pull.off.my						teeth	the.doctor	

'The doctor pulled out my teeth.' [elicited 91.7.17-73]

The choice of a grammatical argument is neither random nor interchangeable: it is governed by the semantic content and semantic role of the possessed argument. In terms of semantic content, the possessed is more likely to be chosen as a grammatical argument (possession marking on the argument) when it is human, especially a kinsman, whereas the choice of the possessor (possession marking on the predicate) is more likely when the possessed is inanimate. In terms of the semantic role, there is an interesting skewing in the subject position: when the possessed subject is highly agentive, the possessed is most often chosen as a grammatical argument; in contrast, when the possessed subject is low in agentivity, the possessor is typically chosen as a grammatical argument. This skewing in the usage patterns is consistent enough to be suggestive, but not enough to constitute a grammaticized pattern. Thus, the choice of a grammatical argument cannot be characterized solely on the basis of either the semantic content or the semantic role of the possessed.

When we examine the discourse characteristics, a striking pattern emerges. There is a very strong correlation between the choice of grammatical argument and the discourse salience of the possessor and the possessed. The possessor is chosen as a grammatical argument when the possessor is more discourse-salient (i.e., more likely to be tracked in discourse) than the possessed. For example, consider example (360) below.

(360)	*ḥayuqˀičḥˀaƛ̓its*	***qʷiyaakiis***	***qaḥšiƛ̓***	***ˀumˀiiqsu*.**
		*qʷiyu -ˀ**a·k** -(y)i:s*	*qaḥ -ši(ƛ̓)*	*ˀumˀi·qsu*
		when -POSS -INDF.1sg	dead -MOM	mother
	I.was.ten.years.old	when.my	died	mother

‘I was ten years old when my mother died.’ [CLLS 17]

Notice that within the predication *qʷiyaakiis qaḥšiƛ̓ ˀumˀiiqsu* ‘when my mother died’ the subject pronominal index of the main predicate *qʷiyu* ‘when’ is coreferential with the possessor. That is, it is the possessor rather than the possessed that is coded as a grammatical argument of the main predicate. This sentence was produced in the context where the speaker is talking about herself at the time of her mother’s death, and therefore the most salient participant is the speaker herself. In fact, in the narrative that follows (360) (not presented here), the speaker proceeds to elaborate on the situation surrounding her, and there is no further mention of her mother. Thus, when we consider the possessed participant *‘my mother’*, the possessor is more discourse-salient than the possessed and is coded as a grammatical argument. A similar correlation can be seen in (361). Observe the argument choice in the predication *ˀans wik̓iituk ˀaˀiičum* ‘because I had no parents’. The pronominal index on the main predicate *ˀan* ‘because’ indicates that the first-person possessor is the subjective argument.

(361)	*ˀuẏiiḥaƛ̓atsa*	*činuqƛ̓ap̓atˀał*	*wałšiƛ̓*
	ˀu -ẏi·ḥa -'aƛ̓ -'at -sa	*činuqƛ̓ -'ap -'at -ˀa·ł*	*wał -ši(ƛ̓)*
	it -being.because.of-TEL -SHIFT-1sg	unwilling -CAUS -SHIFT-PL	go.home -MOM
	because.of.it.they	they.were.unwilling	go.home

ˀans	***wik̓iituk***	***ˀaˀiičum*.**
ˀan -s	*wik̓i:t **-uk***	*DUP- ˀi:čum*
because -1sg	none.present -POSS	DISTR- parent
because.I	there.is.none.present	parents

‘For the reason that I had no parents they didn’t want to let me go home.’ [CLLS 305]

As in (360) the choice of a grammatical argument coincides with the discourse salience of the participants. In (361) the speaker is explaining why the teachers at the residential school she attended did not let her leave the school. The predication in question is about the speaker’s situation rather than about her parents, and in fact, the speaker herself remains to be the topic in the stretch of a narrative that follows (361) (not presented here). Thus, in this context the speaker, i.e., the possessor, is more discourse-salient than her parents, i.e., the possessed, and it is the possessor that is chosen as a grammatical argument.

Compare this with the cases where the possessed is more salient than the possessor.

(362) *ʔuuḥw̓ałʔaƛquu* **ʔumʔiiqsakitqs**
ʔu -ḥw̓ał -'aƛ -qu: *ʔumʔi·qsu* ***-ʔa·k*** *-it -qs*
it -using -TEL -COND.3 mother -POSS -PAST -SUB.1sg
she.would.use.it my.late.mother

k̓ʷiikʷitxsumup *newspaper,*
DUP- *kʷitx -sumup*
glue.on -MOMCAUS
paste.on.the.wall

'My late mother used to use newspaper to line the walls.' [CLLS 39]

(363) *ʔuḥʔaƛquu* ***ʔumʔiiqsakitqsʔał*** *ʔustˤaqƛpiƛ.*
ʔuḥ -'aƛ -qu: *ʔumʔi·qsu* ***-ʔa·k*** *-it -qs -ʔa·ł* *ʔust-ˤaqƛ-pi(ƛ)*
being.she -TEL -COND.3 mother -POSS -PAST -SUB.1sg-PL LOC -?? -being.on.the.floor
it.used.to.be.she my.late.mother.and.others getting.on.the.floor

waa ʔuʔiiʔasʔap *k̓anisʔi* *čumʔiłukʷiʔał.*
wa· ʔu -ʔi: -'as -'ap *k̓anis -ʔi·* *čumʔił -uk -i -ʔa·ł*
and it -getting.to -being.on.the.platform-CAUS stop.over -DEF bed -POSS -??-PL
and put.him.on.the.platform one.staying.over their.bed

'It used to be my late mother and [other relatives] [instead of the visitor] who slept on the floor and gave their bed to the visitor.' [CLLS 51]

Example (362) occurs in a stretch where the speaker tells about how her mother lined the wall of the house. Here, in contrast to (360), the possessed *'mother'* is more discourse-salient than the possessor *'I'*, and it is the possessed that is chosen to serve as a grammatical argument (the possessed third person controls the form of the pronominal suffix on the main predicate *ʔuuḥw̓ał* 'use ...', i.e., Ø). Similarly in (363), the speaker is explaining how well people used to take care of visitors in the old days. Here, it is *'my late mother and others'*, not the speaker herself, that is contrasted with *the people who stay over*, and therefore *'my late mother and others'* is more salient than the speaker herself. Thus, the possessed is more salient than the possessor *'I'*. And again the possessed is chosen to serve as a grammatical argument.

This correlation between discourse salience and possession marking further provides an explanation for skewing of the semantic content and semantic role of the possessed. As described above, the possessed that is human and agent tends to be chosen over the possessor as a grammatical argument. Both humanness and agency are known to correlate with high discourse salience. The skewing based on semantic characteristics, therefore, can be considered part of the discourse-based pattern: when the possessed is potentially high in topicality in terms of semantic characteristics, the possessed tends to be chosen as a grammatical argument.

Thus, the two strategies of marking possession of an argument in Nuuchahnulth involve decisions at the level of argument structure that are based on discourse dynamics.

4.5.3. Perspective-Shifting

Nuuchahnulth has a PERSPECTIVE-SHIFTING suffix -*'at* that affects the semantics of the predicate in such a way that the whole predication is framed in terms of the effect of an action, event, or state.[16] The change is also reflected in the grammatical arrangement of the arguments. In a typical transitive predication, a participant with high agency (ACTOR) occurs as the subject, controlling the subject pronominal suffix, and a participant with low agency (UNDERGOER) occurs as the object.[17] With the PERSPECTIVE-SHIFTING suffix -*'at* the undergoer takes control of the pronominal suffix, while the actor loses the morphological privilege. The changes in grammatical status of the actor and undergoer are illustrated in (364) and (365). In a typical two-participant transitive sentence, the pronominal suffix is coreferential with the actor as in (364), but in a sentence with the suffix -*'at* the pronominal suffix is coreferential with the undergoer as in (365). In terms of the morphological marking on the predicate, the undergoer in the -*'at* sentence is given a special grammatical status that it does not otherwise have, and the actor in the -*'at* sentence lacks the special status that it otherwise has.

---

[16] The suffix -*'at* in Nuuchahnulth has been characterized in the previous literature as a 'passive' or 'inverse' marker. Sapir and Swadesh (Sapir and Swadesh 1939; Swadesh 1933; Sapir 1924) were the first to use the term 'passive' for this suffix, but they provide neither a detailed description of its use nor a justification for calling it 'passive'. In their fairly detailed discussions of uses of the same suffix, Rose (1981) and Rose and Carlson (1984) basically accept the characterization 'passive', but they note deviation of the -*'at* construction from the prototypical syntactic passive. Whistler (1985) proposes an alternative analysis of the suffix as an inverse marker similar to that found in Algonquian languages. Emanatian (1988) makes a counterproposal that the -*'at* construction is in fact a prototypical syntactic passive. I consider both 'passive' and 'inverse' to be inaccurate and misleading characterizations for the Nuuchahnulth -*'at* construction. For detailed discussion, see Nakayama (1997b).

[17] I use the terms ACTOR and UNDERGOER to characterize the two participants that are semantically involved in the transitive predication and differ in relative agency: ACTOR for participant with higher agency and UNDERGOER for that with lower agency. Notice that ACTOR and UNDERGOER are semantic macroroles based on relative agency and are not the equivalents of 'agent' and 'patient' in the narrow senses of these terms. As pointed out by Foley and Van Valin (1984) and Van Valin (1993), not all semantic roles are distinguished in every part of grammar. Rather, a group of roles are treated alike for certain purposes in the grammar. With respect to transitive predications, there are two groups of semantic roles, those with higher agency and those with lower agency: the former are typically expressed as subject simple transitive (neither causativized nor passivized) predicates, while the latter typically occur as objects.

(364) 1 plural (ACTOR) → 2 plural (UNDERGOER)

haaˤanˀaqniš *siiḥaɬ.*
ha:ˤan -ˀaq -niš *si:ḥaɬ*
invite -FUT **-1pl** you.all

'We will invite you all.' [elicited 7.24.91-77]

(365) 3 singular (ACTOR) → 1 singular (UNDERGOER)

haaˤanˀanits.
ha:ˤan **-'at** *-it -s*
invite **-SHIFT** -PAST **-1sg**

'I was invited.'
'He invited me' [elicited 7.24.91-81]

The change in the morphological marking pattern may be linked to syntactic reorganization of sentence structure in some languages, but in Nuuchahnulth there is not enough evidence to prove a structural alignment between morphological marking and syntactic structure. In spite of its special morphological status, the undergoer in the *-'at* construction cannot clearly be differentiated from that in the non-*'at* construction in terms of syntactic privileges. The argument that controls the pronominal suffix in Nuuchahnulth does not necessarily play a major role in the organization of the syntactic structure of a sentence in the way that the 'subject' in European languages does. Thus, the fact that the undergoer gains control over the pronominal suffixing does not have direct implications for the syntactic privileges of the undergoer within the sentence, and therefore it is not reasonable to characterize the grammatical change concerning the undergoer as a 'syntactic promotion'.

4.5.3.1. Types of Effects on the Participant Configuration

The suffix *-'at* can be used in three major ways to affect the pragmatic configuration of participants.

4.5.3.1.1. Perspective Reversal

When the predicate expresses a transitive action with both an animate actor and an animate undergoer, use of *-'at* leads to a shift in perspective. In a prototypical transitive clause the actor is a central participant both morphologically and pragmatically. When the predicate is affixed with *-'at,* however, it is the undergoer that controls the pronominal suffix and is pragmatically at the center of the perspective. In the following examples *us* and *the wife* are the undergoer and the central participant.

(366) *they* (ACTOR) → *us* (UNDERGOER)
ʔuqḥy̓uuʔiɬʔaninaʔaaɬʔaɬ
ʔu -(q)ḥy̓u·　-ʻiɬ　-'at　-(y)ina　-ʔa:ɬ　-ʔa·ɬ
it -being.together -being.in.the.house-SHIFT -INDF.1pl -always-PL
'They used to live with us.' [CLLS 100]

(367) *they* (ACTOR) → *the wife* (UNDERGOER)
kʷiscaʔapʔaƛat　ɬuucmaʔi,
kʷis　-ca　-'ap　-'aƛ -'at　ɬu:cma -ʔi·
be.different -going.to -CAUS -TEL -SHIFT　wife　-DEF
taken.to.a.different.place　the.wife
'They took the wife to a different place.'
'The wife was taken to a different place.' [Kingfisher 36]

The actor in the *-'at* construction is expressed as a nonsubject argument morphologically (which lacks control of the pronominal suffixing on the predicate), but otherwise it is not syntactically distinguishable from the actor in active sentences. It can be expressed as a direct argument.

(368) *m̓ačiʔats　**maackʷin***
*m̓a -či(ƛ) **-'at** -s　ma:ckʷin*
bite -MOM -SHIFT -1sg　mosquito
'I was bitten by a mosquito.'
'A mosquito bit me.' [elicited 7.17.91-44]

(369) *ƛičiʔatƛa　**mamaɬn̓i**.*
*ƛi　-či(ƛ)**-'at**　-ƛa·　mamaɬn̓i*
shoot -MOM -SHIFT -also　white.man
'He was shot at by white men again.'
'White men shot at him again.' [Kingfisher 134]

Rose (1981: 57) proposes that direct actor arguments like *maackʷin* 'mosquito' and *mamaɬn̓i* 'white man' in the above examples in fact have a syntactically peripheral 'oblique' status. Her claim is based on the observation that the actor argument in the *-'at* construction, unlike that in the non-*'at* construction, has limited word-order flexibility: it cannot precede the predicate with which it is associated and does not normally precede the core arguments with which it is associated. However, word-order flexibility alone does not provide strong evidence for a syntactic category, especially in a language where word order is normally flexible and is responsive to pragmatic demands. In fact this constraint can very well be explained pragmatically. As can be independently shown, in Nuuchahnulth discourse information that is salient or contrasted is most likely to be placed in initial position before the predicate. When the *-'at* construction is used in discourse, an actor such as *maackʷin* 'mosquito' or *mamaɬn̓i* 'white man' in the above examples generally occupies a relatively unimportant place within the immediate context. Therefore, it does not make sense to put it into the pragmatically highlighted position, i.e., sentence-initially (before the predicate). This pragmatic explanation is consistent with the general characteristic of Nuuchahnulth as a 'pragmatic word order language' (Thompson 1978), and it seems better to view the word-order flexibility as a factor independent of the syntactic status of an argument. Given the lack of definitive evidence for its syntactic peripherality, it seems most reasonable to conclude that the actor argument in the *-'at* construction is syntactically no less central within the sentence than that in the non-*'at* construction.

Related to the issue of syntactic demotion of the actor is the question of valency in the *-'at* construction. The prototypical passive as defined above involves reduction of the valence of the predicate through removal of the actor from the core argument structure. However, as we have already seen, the Nuuchahnulth *-'at* construction can retain the actor as a direct argument. Although this actor argument does not control the pronominal suffix on the predicate, it is indistinguishable from the actor in non-*'at* sentences in terms of syntactic privileges. Thus, the *-'at* predicate is just as 'transitive' as the non-*'at* form of the predicate. More accurately, the criterion based on valency change cannot be applied to Nuuchahnulth in a meaningful way. Nuuchahnulth grammar is not sensitive to the transitivity of a predicate, that is, there is no grammatical marker in Nuuchahnulth that indicates the transitivity of a predicate. Therefore, any application of the notion of syntactic transitivity to Nuuchahnulth sentence structure is bound to be arbitrary, e.g., based on the number of overtly expressed direct arguments.

The range of participant structures in the two-participant *-'at* construction is constrained in a systematic way. The constraint has been characterized in terms of the animacy hierarchy (see Whistler 1985): the *-'at* construction almost always shows a participant structure where the participant with the lower animacy rank acts on the participant with the higher animacy rank. To look at this constraint from another viewpoint, *-'at* can be used only when the undergoer is higher in animacy than the actor. The hierarchy is laid out in (370).

(370) Animacy hierarchy governing the Nuuchahnulth *-'at* construction:

1, 2 > salient 3 > non-salient 3

What (370) suggests is that the *-'at* construction is required whenever a lower participant acts on a higher participant. That is, the *-'at* construction is not allowed when a first- or second-person participant (speech act participant, SAP) acts on either a third person or another SAP. On the other hand, when a third person acts on a SAP, the sentence must be put into the *-'at* construction. When the sentence does not involve a SAP, the use of the *-'at* construction is governed by the relative discourse salience of the actor and undergoer: the *-'at* construction is not allowed when the discourse-salient participant acts on the nonsalient participant, while it is required when the nonsalient participant acts on the salient participant. This pattern for using of *-'at* is summarized in Table 4.

Table 4: Pattern for Use of *-'at*

Participant Configuration ACTOR → UNDERGOER	Use of ***-'at***
<u>**1, 2**</u> → 3	Prohibited
3 → <u>**1, 2**</u>	Obligatory
1, 2 → 1, 2	Prohibited
<u>**3**</u> → 3'	Prohibited
3' → <u>**3**</u>	Obligatory

Note: Underlining indicates the participant that is higher in animacy

The following excerpt from a text illustrates the use of the *-'at* construction triggered by relative discourse salience of third-person participants. In this excerpt the protagonist, a mink called Kwaaxtii, who killed the wolf chief, is being pursued by packs of wolves that are eager to take revenge. Notice that the *-'at* construction is used in (c) and (d), when peripheral characters, i.e., wolves, are acting on the protagonist Kwaaxtii.

(371) [Mink 165–172]

a. protagonist > peripheral
naˀaaƛ k̓ʷaaxtii,
naˀa:-'aƛ
hear -TEL NAME
heard Kwaaxtii

'Kwaaxtii heard them [the wolves that were howling].'

b. protagonist > peripheral
wik̓aƛ ḥaˀukʷiƛ.
wik-'aƛ ḥaˀu -kʷi(ƛ)
not -TEL respond -MOM
didn't answer.to

'He didn't answer them [the wolves].'

c. peripheral > protagonist
ˀuuktisˀaƛatˀiš k̓ʷaaxtii,
*ˀu -ktis -'aƛ **-'at** -ˀi·š*
it -acting.by.ref.to -TEL -SHIFT -IND.3 NAME
they.are.following.it Kwaaxtii

'They [the wolves] were following Kwaaxtii.'

(1 line omitted)

d. peripheral > protagonist

misp̓uuqsy̓iḥat			*ʔin*	*waw̓ik*
mis -p̓u·qs	*-y̓i·ḥa*	***-'at***	*ʔin*	*wax -'ik*
smell -smelling.of -feeling.too.much		-SHIFT	because	break.wind -one.who.always.does
they.could.smell.him.so.clearly			because	one.who.always.breaks.wind

'They could smell the odor [of Kwaaxtii] so clearly since he kept breaking wind.'

(1 line omitted)

e. protagonist > peripheral

ʔayisaqsiɬaw̓iɬasʔaƛ				*č̓aastimcm̓it.*
ʔayisaq -siɬa		*-w̓iɬas*	*-'aƛ*	*č̓a:stimc -m̓i·t*
deceive -acting.like		-about.to	-TEL	mink -son.of
he.is.going.to.trick				Son.of.Mink

'The Son of Mink [Kwaaxtii] was going to trick them.'

4.5.3.1.2. Undergoer-Centralized Perspective-Setting

The PERSPECTIVE-SHIFTING suffix can be associated with a predicate that would not take the undergoer to express the effect of a nontransitive event or state on the undergoer. Since the undergoer participant is external to the event or state expressed by the base predicate, this use of the suffix *-'at* in effect introduces an additional participant into the event.

(372) *ʔiiḥʔat kʷiisḥii,* cf. *ʔiiḥ kʷiisḥii* 'be very strange' [one-place]

ʔi:ḥʷ ***-'at***	*kʷis*	*-ḥi·*
very -SHIFT	be.strange	-DUR

'People were very strange to him.' [Qawiqaalth 20]

(373) *m̓iƛyuuʔtintiis* cf. *m̓iƛyuu* 'rained, be rainy' [zero-place]

m̓iƛ	*-yu·*	***-'at***	*-int*	*-(y)i:s*
rain	-done	-SHIFT	-PAST	-INDF.1sg

'I got rained on.' (Rose and Carlson 1984: 17a)[18]

The fact that the *-'at* sentence can involve a different set of participants from those associated with the base predicate shows that the *-'at* sentence is not a construction derived from the corresponding construction through the application of a regular

18 This example is from the Kyuquot dialect. However, the dialectal differences do not affect the validity of the example in this context.

syntactic process, unlike the passive construction in English, which can be thought of as derived from the active counterpart through a regular syntactic process.

4.5.3.1.3. Departicularization

The PERSPECTIVE-SHIFTING suffix *-'at* can also be used to express a nonparticularized action or event without a specific actor. Thus, the actor in this DEPARTICULARIZING construction is invariably nonreferential or impersonal. This use of *-'at* is usually observed with predicates that do not involve an undergoer participant. When it is observed with predicates with an undergoer, the undergoer is invariably inanimate and is not discourse-salient in the sense that it does not constitute the entity most likely to be talked about in the given context.

In terms of form, the predicate in a DEPARTICULARIZING *-'at* construction always takes the third-person form, i.e., zero marking. On the basis of parallelism with other uses of the suffix *-'at,* the undergoer participant is expected to control the form of the predicate. However, it is clear that the undergoer does not control the form of the predicate, since, as noted above, the undergoer participant is often not involved in the DEPARTICULARIZING *-'at* construction. Thus, the use of the third-person form in this construction is best considered as grammaticized.

We can distinguish three types of contexts where the DEPARTICULARIZING *-'at* construction is commonly used, i.e., generic statements, instructive expressions, and nonspecific actions.

4.5.3.1.3.1. Generic Statements

The DEPARTICULARIZING *-'at* construction can express generic statements. The prototypical cases involve relatively atemporal predicates, especially states. Here departicularization of the action is realized as atemporality and elimination of a specific agent. In (374) the speaker is describing the distance from her village to Port Alberni, B.C. Notice that the predicate *ṅupčiiɬuk̓ʷat* 'it takes one day' does not involve the undergoer.

(374) *ṅupčiiɬuk̓ʷat.*
ṅup -či·ɬ -uk ***-'at***
one -days.long -DUR -SHIFT
'It took one day [to reach Port Alberni].' [CLLS 216]

Example (375) was produced in a traditional narrative as background generic information to explain the protagonist's action. In the immediately preceding part the protagonist dove into a river and picked up a rock in his hands.

(375)

ƛ̓ay̓ixˀatˀiš		*m̓uksy̓i*	*ˀuqƛn̓uk̓ʷat.*	
*ƛ̓ay̓ix-**'at***	*-ˀi·š*	*m̓uksy̓i*	*ˀuqƛ-n̓uk*	*-'at*
swift -SHIFT	-IND.3	rock	hold?-being.at.hand	-SHIFT
one.is.fast		rock	have.in.hands	

'You can move fast [under water] when you are holding rocks in your hands [as ballast].' [Kingfisher 141]

4.5.3.1.3.2. Instructive Expressions

The DEPARTICULARIZING *-'at* construction can also be used to express advice or instruction. In these uses the departicularization is associated with the generality or nonindividuality of social expectations and obligations shared by all community members. Thus, advice or instruction expressed with *-'at* sentences is based on social expectation, as in 'in our society things are done in this way' or 'people do … this way' rather than on individual authority, as in 'I think you should do so' or 'I order you to do so'. Distributionally, the INSTRUCTIVE *-'at* uses are found with highly controllable, executable actions. They do not occur with predicates that are in irrealis modes such as the conditional (when, if) and predicates that denote uncontrollable actions (cf. examples below in NONSPECIFIC ACTIONS section). The INSTRUCTIVE use significantly overlaps with the NONSPECIFIC use in terms of both distribution and meaning, and may well be considered a specialized case of the NONSPECIFIC use.

The INSTRUCTIVE *-'at* construction is most common when a speaker explains to a the hearer how to perform a certain task. Example (376) occurred in a stretch where the speaker explained how food-gathering used to be done. This example could be interpreted either as the INSTRUCTIVE use or the NONSPECIFIC use.

(376)

huuˀak̓at		*ˀacšiˀat,*	
hu:ˀak	***-'at***	*ˀac*	*-ši(ƛ)-**'at***
early	-SHIFT	go.out.fishing	-MOM -SHIFT
being.early		go.out.fishing	

'You should go out fishing early.'
'People go out fishing early.' [Canoe 92]

The INSTRUCTIVE use is appropriate when the utterance is negative or refers to an immediate action that is about to be performed by the addressee. In (377) the speaker is explaining how to fillet fish.

(377) *ƛuułḥap̓at.*

ƛu:ł	*-(q)ḥ*	*-'ap*	***-'at***
gentle	-SIM	- CAUS	-SHIFT
do.it.slowly			

wik̓at		*wiiškp̓ičḥat*		
wik	***-'at***	*wišk*	*-p̓ičḥ*	***-'at***
not	-SHIFT	scold	-doing.while	-SHIFT
don't		doing.without.care		

'Do it slowly. Don't just do it without care.' [CLLS 115]

4.5.3.1.3.3. Nonspecific Actions

The use of *-'at* for expressing NONSPECIFIC ACTIONS is most clearly observed with instantaneous actions and events.

(378) *ˀuṅaaḥšiˀaƛ̓atquu* *ḥuu* *č̓aˀak.*

ˀu	*-ṅa·ḥ*	*-ši(ƛ)*	*-'aƛ*	***-'at***	*-qu:*	*ḥu:*	*č̓aˀak*
it	-seeking	-MOM	-TEL	-SHIFT	-COND.3	yonder	water
one.would.go.for.it						yonder	water

'Then we would go far looking for fresh water.' [CLLS 74]

(379) *č̓iḥšiˀanit.*

č̓iḥ	*-ši(ƛ)*	***-'at***	*-it*
supernatural	-MOM	-SHIFT	-PAST

'Something unusual happened.' [Dog 2]

The meaning and distribution of this NONSPECIFIC use overlap with those of the INSTRUCTIVE type discussed above, but the former is found in wider contexts. The NONSPECIFIC use, but not the INSTRUCTIVE use, can be found in irrealis, conditional sentences like (380) and (381).

(380) *ṅiƛaak̓aƛ̓atquu.*

ṅiƛa:k	*-'aƛ*	***-'at***	*-qu:*
fight	-TEL	-SHIFT	-COND.3

'If you quarrel, [you become a snail].' [CLLS 185]

(381) *ˀuuḥc̓iiẇiłasˀaƛ̓atquu* *łuḥc̓iti*

ˀu	*-ḥc̓i·*	*-ẇiłas*	*-'aƛ*	***-'at***	*-qu:*	*łuḥc̓iti*
it	-holding.over.fire	-about.to	-TEL	-SHIFT	-COND.3	head

'When you cook the fish heads, [you leave some meat on the heads].' [CLLS 149]

The NONSPECIFIC use also differs from the INSTRUCTIVE use in that it can describe uncontrollable events.

(382) *łaakłaak̓ʷat,* *wikp̓iˤatquu,*
REDUP-*ła:kʷ* **-'at** *wik-p̓iq* **-'at** *-qu:*
please.do -SHIFT not -?? -SHIFT -COND.3
please.do so.nothing.would.happen

wik̓atquu *ˀuusuqtat,*
wik-**'at** *-qu:* *ˀu:suqta*-**'at**
not -SHIFT -COND.3 hurt -SHIFT
may.nothing.happen one.gets.hurt

'May there not be an accident.' [Canoe 7]

4.5.3.2. The Nature of the Effects of the Perspective-Shifting

Use of the suffix *-'at* has a major effect on the pragmatic and morphological configuration of participants within a sentence. In terms of effects on the participant configuration, the suffix *-'at* shows a partial resemblance to grammatical voice systems in other languages. However, it is not appropriate to compare the use of *-'at* in Nuuchahnulth to a grammaticized voice alternation. First, the effect of *-'at* on the grammatical structure of a sentence is not very well defined. For example, the undergoer could be considered to be grammatically promoted from the nonsubject status to subject in the *-'at* construction (see the perspective reversing type described in 4.5.3.1.3.1). But this applies only to transitive predicates, not to the *-'at* constructions for which 'active' counterparts do not exist (see the undergoer-centralizing and departicularizing types described in 4.5.3.1.3.2 and 4.5.3.1.3.3.). To give another example, in most cases the undergoer is expressed as the subject in the *-'at* construction. But again, this is not always the case (see the departicularizing type). Thus, the formal effects of *-'at* are too varied to warrant a view of it as a regular grammaticized alternation in the sentence structure.

Another respect in which *-'at* differs from grammatical voice systems is in the structural environment, i.e., the network of structural alternations the construction is involved in. Unlike a grammaticized voice alternation, the apparent structural alternation involving the *-'at* construction is not completely regular: as is evident in the uses of the undergoer-centralizing type and the departicularizing type, there are *-'at* constructions where the set of participants involved is not identical to the non-*'at* constructions based on the same predicate. Thus, the *-'at* construction is structurally independent: that is, it cannot be derived from other constructions through a regular structural operation. (See Rose 1981: 80ff. §3.3.1.1 and Rose and Carlson 1984 for a similar observation.)

These observations suggest that the function of *-'at* is fundamentally different from that of a marker of a grammaticized voice alternation, regardless of some similarities in surface effects. The primary function of *-'at* is not a grammaticized rearrangement of a given sentence structure. The participant configuration that is unique to the *-'at* construction cannot result from a regular structural rearrangement of some other construction; rather it is built anew based on the *-'at* predicate. Thus, the function of *-'at* is more lexico-semantic than structural: i.e., *-'at* is used to affect the semantics of the predicate in such a way that the whole predication is framed in terms of the (direct or indirect) effect of an event or state. This semantic characterization correctly captures the facts that the effect of the suffix *-'at* is not grammatically well defined and that use of a non-*'at* construction cannot be characterized as a regular structural alternation.

This general semantic function is realized in two ways: it results in the predication being (i) projected from the undergoer's perspective or (ii) departicularized in the sense that it is unspecified for a particular agent. The distribution of the two types of semantic effects is systematic. Use of *-'at* leads to a perspective shift if the predicate expresses a transitive action with both an animate actor and an animate undergoer. This change is reflected in the pragmatic configuration of participants as a centralized undergoer and a decentralized actor. The suffix *-'at* also causes a perspective shift when the predicate expresses an event that does not involve an undergoer, such as a meteorological event. In this case the change in the discourse participant structure involves the introduction of the undergoer participant that is not among the participants associated with the base predicate (the non-*'at* form of the predicate). When *-'at* is used on the predicate without an animate undergoer, the *-'at* construction expresses nonspecific predication. In terms of the discourse participant structure, the actor is removed from the structure.

4.6. Patterns of Encoding of the Participant Configuration in Discourse

How an event or state and the configuration of participants in the physical world are encoded in discourse is not inherently determined. The speaker can easily choose to encode the same state of affairs in the physical world in different ways according to the requirements at a particular point in discourse. Thus the choice of encoding strategies is very much a matter of discourse dynamics. In this section I discuss two major encoding decisions that Nuuchahnulth speakers face: (i) morphological vs. syntactic encoding of participants, and (ii) a simplex vs. complex predication.

4.6.1. Morphological vs. Syntactic Encoding of Participants

Because of the unusually powerful derivational possibilities offered by lexical suffixes, information that might be contained in a full sentence in English can be expressed morphologically in Nuuchahnulth. Thus, there is an overlap between what can be encoded in morphology and what can be encoded in syntax. In other words, the same information can sometimes be encoded either morphologically or syntactically. This overlap in encodability raises an interesting question about the functional difference between the encoding strategies: that is, why the speaker chooses one strategy of encoding over the other. In this section I consider that question, focusing on the encoding of participants.

A single semantic configuration of participants can be encoded in very different forms: either morphologically within a predicative word as a root or syntactically as a separate argument. In the following examples, the participant *child* is expressed either morphologically as a root (383) or syntactically as an argument (384).

(383)	*t̓aatn̓anakšiƛ̓ˀaƛquuk*	*waaˀaƛ̓ats.*
	t̓a:tn̓a *-na·k -ši(ƛ)-'aƛ -qu:k*	*wa:-'aƛ -'at -s*
	children -having-MOM -TEL -COND.2sg	say -TEL -SHIFT-1sg
	when.you.get.children	it.was.said.to.me

'when you have children' [CLLS 130]

(384)	*ˀunaakˀaɬ*	***t̓aatn̓a.***
	ˀu -na·k -ˀa·ɬ	*t̓a:tn̓a*
	it -having-PL	children
	they.have.them	children

'They had children.' [GLLS 3]

My textual study suggests that the key factor in choosing one strategy over the other is the referentiality of a nominal concept.[19] A predicate with a morphologically expressed nominal concept tends to express habitual, institutionalized activities rather than particular ones. The predicate in (383) above expresses a general activity of *having children* rather than a particular activity bound in time and place (e.g., having a particular child). Thus, a nominal concept expressed within a complex predicative word, like *t̓aatn̓a* 'children' in (383), is not referential in discourse (not used for introducing and tracking a referent in discourse). In contrast, a nominal concept that is expressed as a syntactic argument is used referentially. Observe the contrast between (a) and (b) below.

(385)

a. *č̓aapaciiɬw̓it̓as.*
č̓apac *-i:ɬ -w̓it̓as*
canoe -making -about.to
about.to.make.a.canoe

'He is going to make a canoe.' [Canoe 1]

---

[19] A similar observation has been made for the use of lexical suffixes in neighboring Salishan languages (Egesdal 1981).

b. *6 months* *hił* *p̓aačiina* *č̓apac* *ʔusiik*
hił *p̓a:či:na* ***č̓apac*** *ʔu -si:k*
be.there Pachina canoe it -completing

'For six months, I was at Pachina completing the canoe.' [GLLS 138]

Sentence (385a) was produced at the beginning of a narrative in which the speaker explained how a canoe used to be built. Here *canoe* is part of a generic action of *canoe-making,* and therefore the root *č̓apac* 'canoe' does not refer to a particular entity. In (385b) the same root *č̓apac,* which is expressed as a separate word in this case, is used referentially to make reference to a particular canoe that the speaker was requested to build. A similar contrast is observed in the following pair of examples.

(386)

a. context: They [my grandparents and parents] told me to have sons.
ʕuy̓iič̓ap̓at, *hitaaqƛiƛ.*
ʕuy̓i *-'i·c* *-'ap* *-'at* *hita* *-'a·qƛi(ƛ)*
medicine -consuming -CAUS -SHIFT get.there -being.in.the.woods
made.me.take.medicine go.into.a.forest

'They had me take medicine in the woods [so that I could have sons].' [CLLS 328]

b. *sukʷiʔaƛ* *ʕuy̓aakʔi*
sukʷi(ƛ) -'aƛ ***ʕuy̓i*** *-ʔa·k -ʔi·*
take -TEL medicine -POSS -DEF
took his.medicine

'He [Mink] took out his medicine [to create a lake].' [Mink 177]

In (386a) *ʕuy̓i* 'medicine' is part of a general activity of medicine-taking and therefore does not refer to a particular medicine. In contrast, *ʕuy̓i* in (386b) does refer to a particular medicine owned by Mink as indicated by the possessive and definite suffixes. Examples (383) and (384) discussed on page 144 also show the parallel contrast.

Although very different in structural terms, lexical suffixation and the phenomenon of noun incorporation show a great deal of functional similarity in this aspect. As has been pointed out in the literature (Sapir 1911b: 259; Mithun 1984: 866, 890; Hopper and Thompson 1984), the incorporated nouns are in contrast with syntactically expressed nouns in that the former tends to be used nonreferentially and the latter referentially.

4.6.2. Simplex vs. Complex Predication

When the same participant structure can be expressed by a simplex predication based on a single clause and by a complex predication based on multiple clauses, it is the discourse characteristics of the undergoer participant that determine the choice of a form of a predication. If the identity of the undergoer needs to be emphasized in order to be either disambiguated from or put in contrast with other entities, the undergoer is expressed in a clause separate from the clause expressing the main event. In other words, a predication takes a complex form consisting of multiple clauses when the undergoer is contextually salient. Observe the examples in (387). Sentences (387a) and (387b) occur next to each other in the text. The simplex predication *naqsaap̓aƛat* 'they were served something to drink' in (387a) and the complex predication *ˀuˀiic̓ap̓at naqšiƛ* 'they were served … to drink' in (387b) refer to the same participants. But the complex form is used when the undergoer's identity is emphasized: in (387b) the undergoer *tea* is contrasted with another type of beverage mentioned in the previous sentence.

(387)

a.

naqsaap̓aƛatquuč̓ˀał,	***č̓aˀak.***
naq -sa·p -'aƛ -'at -qu: -č -ˀa·ł	*č̓aˀak*
drink -MOMCAUS-TEL -SHIFT -COND.3 -INF -PL	water
they.were.given.to.drink	water

'They [white men] served them [native people] water.' [Kingfisher 22]

b.

ˀuušyuuyaƛ	*ˀaḥˀaa,* ***tea,***	***ˀuˀiic̓ap̓at,***	***naqšiƛ.***
ˀu:š -yu:ya -'aƛ	*ˀaḥˀa:*	*ˀu -'i·c -'ap -'at*	*naq -ši(ƛ)*
some -being.at.the.time -TEL	that	it -comsuming -CAUS -SHIFT	drink -MOM
sometimes	they	they.were.served.it	drink

'Sometimes it was tea that they [white men] served them [native people] to drink.' [Kingfisher 23]

This correlation between the discourse salience of the undergoer and a complex form of predication is part of a general antipathy in Nuuchahnulth against expressing more than one direct argument in a clause, especially when the referents are contextually important and most likely to be tracked through discourse. The following are additional examples. Simple predications in (a) and complex predications in (b) involve the same participant structure, but the complex forms in (b) are used when the identity of the undergoer needs to be emphasized.

(388)

a.

wiks	***łačiƛ***	*tič̓imˀakqs.*
wik -s	*łač -i(ƛ)*	*tič̓im -ˀa·k -qs*
not -1sg	let.go-MOM	herb -POSS -SUB.1sg
I.didn't	let.go	my.herbs

'I did not let go of my herbs.' [Wolf 205]

b.

wik	***łačiƛ***		*David Frank*	***ʔuukʷił.***
wik	*łač*	*-i(ƛ)*		*ʔu -kʷił*
not	let.go-MOM			it -being.with.ref.to
not	leave.alone			with.ref.to.him

'He never left David Frank.' [CLLS 71]

(389)

a.

hitinqisʔaƛquu,					***ḥaačałuk***	*łaatḥaʔis.*
hita	*-inq*	*-'is*	*-'aƛ*	*-qu:*	*ḥač-'ałuk*	*ła:tḥa -ʔis*
get.there	-being.down.a.slope	-being.on.the.beach	-TEL	-COND.3	see -looking.after	children-DIM
she.would.go.down.to.the.beach					watch.over	children

'She [the grandmother] would go down to the beach to watch over children.' [CLLS 87]

b.

hiłḥiis			***ḥaacsa***	*łaatḥaʔis,*	***ʔuuʔaałuk.***
hił	*-ḥi·*	*-'is*	*ḥa:csa*	*ła:tḥa -ʔis*	*ʔu -'a·łuk*
be.there	-being.down.a.slope	-being.on.the.beach	see	children -DIM	it -looking.after
be.down.on.the.beach			see	children	looking.after.them

'She would stay down on the beach to watch over the children.' [CLLS 89]

As mentioned above, there is a strong antipathy in Nuuchahnulth against associating more than one direct argument with a predicate. Generally, only one participant is expressed as a direct argument of a predicate even when there are more possible in the context that could be expressed as its direct argument. When more than one participant needs to be expressed overtly for disambiguation or emphasis, the situation of having a clause with multiple direct arguments is sometimes avoided by splitting participants into multiple clauses based on the same predicate. For example, in (390) the actor *ƛaʔuukʷiʔatḥ* 'Clayoquot people' and the undergoer *minwaaʔathʔi* 'the British soldiers' in a single event are separated into two clauses based on the same predicate *hinaačiƛ* 'went out to meet'.

(390)

hinaačiʔaƛ			*ƛaʔuukʷiʔatḥ.*
hin	***-a·či(ƛ)***	*-'aƛ*	
get.there	-going.out.to.meet	-TEL	NAME
went.out.to.meet			Clayoquot
			ACTOR

hinaačiƛ,		*minwaaʔathʔi.*
hin	***-a·či(ƛ)***	*minwa:ʔath -ʔi·*
get.there	-going.out.to.meet	British.soldiers -DEF
went.out.to.meet		the.British.soldiers
		UNDERGOER

'Clayoquots went [in their canoes] out to the sea to meet the British soldiers.' [Kingfisher 192]

The following are additional examples of the construction.

(391)

sukʷiƛ,	*ḥaw̓iłuk*	*ƛaʔuukʷiʔatḥ,*
sukʷi(ƛ)	*ḥaw̓ił -uk*	
take	chief -POSS	NAME
take	their.chief	Clayoquot
	ACTOR	

...

sukʷiƛ,	*miimixt.*
sukʷi(ƛ)	
take	NAME
take	
	UNDERGOER

'The Clayoquot chief took Miimixt.' [Kingfisher 196]

(392)

čaṅiiʔat	*quuʔas*	*ṅaacsa,*
čaṅi: -'at	*qu:ʔas*	*ṅa:csa*
not.seeing -SHIFT	person	see
couldn't.be.recognized	people	see
	ACTOR	

čaṅiiʔat	*čaastimcṁit.*
čaṅi: -'at	*ča:stimc-ṁi·t*
not.seeing -SHIFT	mink -son.of
couldn't.be.recognized	Son.of.Mink
	UNDERGOER

'Son of Mink realized that people couldn't see him.' [Mink 19]

4.7. The Ordering of Arguments

In Greenbergian terms (Greenberg 1963), the 'basic word order' in Nuuchahnulth is VSO. However, this characterization is not very useful; and it may even be misleading for purposes of capturing and explaining the dynamism that shapes syntactic patterns in Nuuchahnulth. Within the Greenbergian framework, the 'basic word order' is determined by the order of constituents in the 'basic' clause, i.e., the pragmatically neutral, main, declarative, affirmative, active clause with a maximum number of overt arguments. The notions of 'basic clause' and 'basic word order', however, are not universally valid (see Mithun 1987; Payne 1987). As noted in the previous section, predications with two overt arguments are extremely rare in actual discourse in Nuuchahnulth, as in other languages. Thus, if we accept that frequency in discourse has at least some place in the discussion of 'basicness' of word order, it does not seem to make good sense to characterize the basic word order in Nuuchahnulth in terms of the clause structure with two overt arguments.

4.7.1. Relative Ordering within a Clause

In Nuuchahnulth discourse it is very unusual for all arguments that are semantically associated with the predicate to be expressed overtly. In a small sample of 734 clauses from three narrative texts, more than half of the predicates occur without any argument, and only 3.8 percent (or 29) of the predicates have two overt arguments: more specifically, V 52.2 percent, VO 20 percent, VS 16.8 percent, OV 5.7 percent, others (VSO, VOS, SV, VOO, OSV) 5.3 percent. Jacobsen (1993) and Rose (1981: 179–182) report similar findings.

4.7.1.1. Ordering between Argument and Predicate

When occurring with arguments, predicates predominantly precede their arguments (predicate–argument 84.9 percent, argument–predicate 15.1 percent). The argument tends to precede the predicate when it carries discourse-salient information, including a focus of contrast, newsworthy information, or a participant whose identity needs disambiguation. For example, in the third utterance in the exchange presented as (393) below, information expressed by the argument (*maaqtusiis*) is the target of the question and therefore is salient in this context. The argument is placed before the predicate.

(393) [CLLS 1–2]

Speaker A: *waastmałitk,*
wa:st -mał   -it   -k
where -being.born -PAST -2sg
'Where were you born?'

Speaker B: *maaqtusiis.*
maaqtusiis
NAME

maaqtusiis *hiistmałits.*
maaqtusiis   hist   -mał   -it   -s
NAME   get.there -being.born -PAST -1sg
'Maaqtusiis. I was born in Maaqtusiis.'

In (394) the argument ʔ*aya łaatńaʔis* 'many children' is contrasted with the speaker himself and placed in initial position.

(394) [GLLS 40–42]
ʔaya* *ƛ̓aatn̓aʔis *ʔuušy̓aʔaƛquu*
ʔaya *ƛ̓a:tn̓a -ʔis* *ʔu:š -y̓a -'aƛ -qu:*
many children -DIM some -being.troubled.by -TEL -COND.3
many children would.have.a.hard.time

wiwik̓ap
DUP- wik -'ap
DISTR- not -CAUS
didn't.do

'Many children had a hard time [at school, because] they didn't understand [English].'

naʔaaƛ̓animts *qʷiyuyiis* *ʔaʔim* *ƛiisƛiisšiƛ*
naʔa:t -'at -imt -s *qʷiyu -(y)i:s* *ʔaʔim* *ƛi:sƛi:s -ši(ƛ)*
understand -SHIFT -PAST -1sg when -INDF.1sg be.first go.to.school -MOM
I.sort.of.understood whenever.I at.first started.school

'I sort of understood [English] when I first went to school.'

In (395) the initial argument *tuškuuḥ* 'ling cod' represents newsworthy information.

(395) *ʔacyuuʔaƛqin* *suuḥaa,*
ʔac -yu· -'aƛ -qʷin *su:ḥa:*
go.out.fishing -done -TEL -COND.1p spring.salmon
when.we.were.out.fishing spring.salmon

ʔuʔuʔiiḥ *cuw̓it,*
ʔu -'i:ḥ *cuw̓it*
it -pursuing coho.salmon
pursuing.it coho.salmon

tuškuuḥ *ʔuušyuuya* *ʔuqs*
tušku:ḥ *ʔu:š -yu:ya* *ʔu -qs*
ling.cod some -being.at.the.time it -being.in.a.vessel
ling.cod sometimes catch.it

'We used to go out fishing for spring salmon and coho. Sometimes we got cod.' [GLLS 45–46]

4.7.1.2. Ordering between Arguments

The preferred order between the subject and object is rather difficult to determine. Although SO order seems to slightly prevail, the number of predications with both S and O is so low (29, or 3.8 percent of the sample of 734 clauses) that it is not clear how strong the tendency is. In fact, Sapir (1924) indicates that OS order is more common: 'Verb, object, subject — this is the most common Nootka order' (p. 83, fn. 4).

4.7.2. The Domain of Argument Placement

An argument is usually placed adjacent to the predicate with which it is associated (or adjacent to another argument that is associated with the same predicate). In other words, an argument typically changes position only within the immediate clause. However, the domain of word-order variation is not necessarily bound to the clause. Although relatively infrequent, arguments in a complex predication consisting of multiple clauses can be deployed with reference to the whole complex predication. To state this from another point of view, a complex predication consisting of serialized clauses can form a single domain of word-order variation. This observation, combined with the fact that such word-order variation does not reach beyond the boundary of a predication, provides another piece of evidence that a predication consisting of serialized clauses forms a structural domain and is structurally different from combination of predications, i.e., COMBINING (see section 4.4.2.1).

This type of long-distance displacement of an argument is typically used to reestablish a discourse-salient referent and to emphasize the identity of a referent either to contrast with other entities, to disambiguate the referent, or to indicate that the identity of the referent is surprising.

The following is a case where the subject is separated from the predicate it is associated with: *qawiqaał*, the subject of the first predicate *wikiłḥ* 'not at home', is placed after the second predicate *kaƛḥšiƛ* 'become daylight'. Here the subject was displaced to the predication-final position to reestablish the protagonist Qawiqaalth as the central participant at the beginning of a new scene.

(396)

Context:
Qawiqaalth said to his mother, 'Listen carefully. I will leave when the moon starts to wax.' His mother listened carefully. She knew he had something unusual in mind. There were many young people in the village, but they kept acting mean to him [Qawiqaalth]. [scene boundary]

wikiłḥ		*kaƛḥšiƛ*		***qawiqaał***.
wik-'ił	*-(q)ḥ*	*kaƛḥ*	*-ši(ƛ)*	*qawiqa:ł*
not -being.in.the.house	-SIM	daylight	-MOM	Qawiqaalth
not.at.home		it.became.daylight		Qawiqaalth
PREDICATE				**ARGUMENT**

'Qawiqaalth was gone when daylight came.' [Qawiqaalth 34]

In the examples below the object argument is separated from the predicate it is associated with. In (397) the object *qʷišaa* 'tobacco' is placed at the end of the predication separate from the predicate *ˀuyiˀaƛatquuč* 'they used to give me'. This utterance occurs in a stretch of narrative where the speaker is quoting an old Nuuchahnulth man who was captured by the British navy. The old man is bragging about the incident where he was served a beverage with tobacco (probably tea leaves) in it, which he was courageous enough to drink. Here the argument displacement was used to present the identity of the referent *qʷišaa* 'tobacco' as a surprising fact.

(397) ***ˀuyiˀaƛatquuč*** *naqsaap̓at,*
ˀu -yi -'aƛ -'at -qu: -č *naq -sa·p -'at*
it -giving -TEL -SHIFT -COND.3 -INF drink -MOMCAUS -SHIFT
they.used.to.give.him serve.a.drink
PREDICATE

qʷišaa.
qʷiš -(y)a·
smoking -CONT
tabacco
ARGUMENT

'They made me drink tobacco.' [Kingfisher 214]

Example (398) is also a case of displacement of the object to predication-final position. This utterance occurs in a scene where a group of top hunters are trying to rescue a young man taken by wolves by slightly injuring him. The fact that the hunters are aiming at the young man's shoulder is significant here. As later explained by the narrator, it is a common practice among Nuuchahnulth people to shoot at the shoulder when they want to capture a person without a major injury, and the hunters are understood to be trying to capture the young man safely rather than trying to injure him. Thus, the identity of the object argument 'shoulder' in (398) is highlighted in this context.

(398) ***ˀuˀiip̓aƛatukitwaˀiš*** *c̓axšiˀat*
ˀuˀi:p -'aƛ -'at -uk -it -wa·ˀi·š *c̓axʷ -ši(ƛ)-'at*
aim.at? -TEL -SHIFT -DUR -PAST -QUOT.3 spear -MOM - SHIFT
there.they.aim.at spear
PREDICATE

ˀaˀapyimłˀatˀi.
ˀap -yimł -'at -ˀi·
LOC -being.on.the.shoulder-POSS -DEF
his.shoulder
ARGUMENT

'They speared at him, aiming at his shoulder.' [Wolf 162]

Long-distance displacement is not limited to rightward movement. In (399) below, in contrast to the above examples, the object argument is placed at the predication-initial position away from its predicate at the end. Such leftward long-distance displacement of an argument appears to have functions that are parallel to fronting within the domain of a clause, i.e., to express newsworthy information, information that is to be contrasted with other information, or information that needs to be disambiguated. The displaced argument *tuškuuḥ* 'ling cod' in (399) represents newsworthy information.

(399)	***tuškuuḥ***	*ˀuušyuuya*	***ˀuqs***
	tušku:ḥ	*ˀu:š -yu:ya*	*ˀu -qs*
	ling.cod	some -being.at.the.time	it -being.in.a.vessel
	ling.cod	sometimes	catch.it
	ARGUMENT		**PREDICATE**

'[We used to go out fishing for spring salmon and coho.] Sometimes we got cod.' [GLLS 46]

Afterword

In this work, I have described the nature of syntactic structuring and the syntactic patterns observed in natural discourse data. As I have shown, Nuuchahnulth has a number of structural characteristics that are relatively unusual, especially in comparison with what we have learned to expect in well-studied languages. These unusual structural characteristics of Nuuchahnulth show how deeply languages can differ. This is of course not to deny the validity and value of searching for universals in human languages, but at the same time a failure to recognize this depth of difference can lead to a misunderstanding of the nature of both individual languages and human language in general. In order to attain a fully accurate understanding of the workings of individual languages, we need to situate observable facts in the context of general structural characteristics. And in order to understand fully the general characteristics of human languages, we need to have an accurate assessment of how profoundly human languages can differ.

Not too surprisingly, many of the unusual aspects of Nuuchahnulth clause and sentence structure are rooted in the unique typological characteristics of the Nuuchahnulth word. In particular, lexical categories are notoriously elusive, and the internal structure of words can be extremely complex. Thanks to numerous lexical suffixes, Nuuchahnulth words can have a highly complex internal structure. In fact, the inventory of lexical suffixes enables speakers to express information either morphologically or syntactically that in English can only be conveyed syntactically. Thus, in the domain of encodable meanings, there is an overlap between morphology and syntax in Nuuchahnulth. When similar information can be expressed either morphologically or syntactically, the choice of encoding strategy depends largely on discourse considerations (see section 4.6.1): thus, a nonreferential or backgrounded, nonsalient participant is typically expressed morphologically as part of a predicate, whereas a referential, salient participant is typically expressed syntactically as a separate argument.

Nuuchahnulth word classes play a major role in shaping the general characteristics of syntactic structuring. The word is syntactically very versatile, and therefore it is difficult to speak of word classes in terms of a narrow range of syntactic functions inherently associated with them (see 3.1). The word-class distinctions that we could identify in Nuuchahnulth grammar are based on functional and behavioral propensities that seem to have been shaped in the intersection between the semantic properties of the word and discourse dynamics. In this sense word classes in Nuuchahnulth are discourse-semantic rather than purely structural (morphological or syntactic) in nature. Also they are not very specialized. The identifiable word classes represent functional and behavioral prototypes (see Rosch 1973) rather than discrete categories, and therefore the boundaries between classes are fuzzy. Although, strictly speaking, most linguistic categories in any language are fuzzy categories, the difficulty in speaking of clear categoriality is much more prominent in Nuuchahnulth word classes than in the lexical category systems of well-studied languages. This discourse-semantic nature and the low specialization of word classes seem to go hand in hand with what we observed about the syntactic structure of Nuuchahnulth, in particular the relatively weak grammaticization on the level of syntax and the fact that the clause does not play as important a role as it does in English.

Word classes in Nuuchahnulth, unlike lexical categories in English, do not represent grammatical primitives in terms of which the higher-level structuring (i.e., syntactic structuring) can be characterized or described. This fact, combined with the lack of a rigid and elaborate system of grammaticized categories and markers that directly refer to syntactic configuration and categories, seems to define one of the fundamental characteristics of Nuuchahnulth syntax. Many aspects of syntactic patternings in Nuuchahnulth are not strongly grammaticized. They are not directly anchored to and cannot be accounted for solely by structural categories, configurations, or constraints.

In order to attain an accurate account of Nuuchahnulth syntax, it is important to take into consideration the nature of the structural environment when drawing conclusions from the observed patterns. Failure to do so can lead to incomplete or distorted accounts of the structural dynamics of the language. For example, if we limit our attention to structural patterns that are directly anchored to grammatical markers, we may get the impression that Nuuchahnulth syntax is extremely fluid or elusive. We might even conclude that there is not much syntactic structure in Nuuchahnulth. Such a view would lead to an impoverished account of Nuuchahnulth syntax. As we have already observed, there are regular patterns and alternations in Nuuchahnulth syntax. By insisting on grammatical anchoring and refusing to consider ungrammaticized behavioral patterns, we would miss the regularities and systematicity of Nuuchahnulth syntax. On the other hand, if we hastily compare these ungrammaticized behavioral patterns to grammatically anchored structural patterns in other languages and apply theoretical devices that are tuned to patterns of the latter type to the ungrammaticized patterns in Nuuchahnulth, we would misrepresent the nature of Nuuchahnulth syntactic patterns by overstructuring the patterns. Even if such a purely structural account did appear to capture satisfactorily the surface patterns, it still falsely suggests that the observed patterns can be recognized and accounted for in purely structural terms (i.e., solely on the basis of structural categories, configuration, and constraints). Thus, it seems clear that the general basis for syntactic patterning is another point of typological variability. Then what appear to be 'same' patterns may be characterized differently depending on the structural environments of a language. This point is of critical importance especially if the goal includes describing the whole structural dynamics of a language.

In Nuuchahnulth, there is not a strong basis for framing the patterns or alternations in a syntactic arrangement of words in purely structural terms. Instead, general syntactic organization is framed more in semantic or discourse-pragmatic terms. Therefore, when there is an option, it is more appropriate to characterize the syntactic regularities in Nuuchahnulth in semantic or discourse-pragmatic terms. For example, the PERSPECTIVE-SHIFTING suffix *-'at* could be characterized by its effect on the grammatical subject as 'a grammatical device for manipulating the subject' or in relation to the discourse-pragmatic configuration of participants as 'a discourse-pragmatic device for indicating the discourse salient participant' (see section 4.5.3). Given the general characteristics of syntactic structuring in Nuuchahnulth, the discourse-pragmatic characterization is more strongly motivated and appropriate as a primary characterization. Note that this conclusion is dependent on the general typological characteristics of the language. Thus, in a language with a different set of typological characteristics, an appropriate characterization of a similar phenomenon may very well be different.

The structural domain of the clause is often observed to play a special, central role in syntactic structuring. But both the role of the clause in syntactic structuring and the nature of clause-level structure are hardly invariable crosslinguistically. Since the definition of 'clause' may vary across different descriptive or theoretical traditions, it can be difficult to make a direct comparison of 'clauses' in different languages. Nonetheless, as a domain defined by a single predicate and its direct arguments, the clause shows crosslinguistic variability in its structural and functional characteristics (see Nichols and Woodbury 1985). The clause in Nuuchahnulth is very different from that in some well-studied languages like English. Within the English clause a very elaborate set of grammatical distinctions (lexical and structural) exist. Thanks to these grammaticized distinctions, English clauses can have a highly complex, hierarchical internal structure. In contrast, grammatical distinctions within a Nuuchahnulth clause are minimal. Nuuchahnulth clauses rarely show an internal structure much more complicated than [PREDICATE + DIRECT ARGUMENTS].

This difference in the characteristics of the internal structure of a clause seems to have a correlation with a difference in the way a complex syntactic construction is built. In English, complex encoding demands can often be accommodated within a clause, whereas in Nuuchahnulth the speaker typically resorts to a combination of multiple clauses. Expressions of temporal notions serve as a good example. In English a temporal notion can be expressed with a prepositional phrase or an adverb within a clause, but in Nuuchahnulth it is typically expressed with a combination of clauses (see examples (259)–(263) on p. 103f.).

Thus, the structural domain of a clause in English is more flexible and can accommodate a wider range of discourse needs. This makes a clause in English more likely to be utilized in discourse to encode single events. The domain of a clause in Nuuchahnulth is less flexible structurally and therefore does not interact as directly with discourse needs as a clause in English. Instead, in Nuuchahnulth, the discourse encoding of an event is more closely associated with the PREDICATION. Thus, syntactic structuring and discourse-semantic event structure interact at different structural domains in different languages.

It seems clear that the range and depth of typological variation in syntactic structuring is much larger than it has often been assumed to be. As discussed above, the nature of syntactic regularities cannot be assumed to be constant across languages, and 'basic' syntactic concepts like 'clause' and 'argument structure' have strong typological implications. It is the relatively uncommon characteristics of Nuuchahnulth that reveal the new sets of typological variables. The more we know about typological variability, the closer we get to a realistic and functionally motivated account of individual languages and human language in general. In other words, an encounter with different types of languages refines our account. In this sense, language diversity is something we cannot afford to lose.

References

Anderson, Stephen R. 1984. Kwakwala Syntax and the Government-Binding Theory. In Eung-Do Cook and Donna B. Gerdts (eds.), Syntax and Semantics 16: The Syntax of Native American Languages, pp. 21–75. New York: Academic Press.

———. 1992. A-Morphous Morphology. Cambridge: Cambridge University Press.

Arima, Eugene Y. 1983. The West Coast (Nootka) People. British Columbia Provincial Museum Special Publication. Victoria, B.C.: British Columbia Provincial Museum.

Arima, Eugene Y., and John Dewhirst. 1990. Nootkans of Vancouver Island. In Wayne Suttles (ed.), Handbook of North American Indians, Vol. 7: Northwest Coast, pp. 391–411. Washington, D.C.: Smithsonian Institution.

Boas, Franz. 1911. Introduction. In Franz Boas (ed.), Handbook of American Indian Languages, Part I, pp. 1–83. Bureau of American Ethnology, Bulletin 40. Washington, D.C.: Government Printing Office.

———. 1947. Kwakiutl Grammar, with a Glossary of the Suffixes. Transactions of the American Philosophical Society 37(3): 201–377.

Chafe, Wallace. 1987. Cognitive Constraints on Information Flow. In Russel Tomlin (ed.), Coherence and Grounding in Discourse, pp. 21–51. Amsterdam: John Benjamins.

Drucker, Philip. 1951. The Northern and Central Nootkan Tribes. Bureau of American Ethnology Bulletin 144, Part 1, pp. 1–480.

Du Bois, John W. 1985. Competing Motivations. In John Haiman (ed.), Iconicity in Syntax, pp. 343–365. Amsterdam: John Benjamins.

Durie, Mark. 1988. Verb Serialization and 'Verbal-Prepositions' in Oceanic Languages. Oceanic Linguistics 27(1/2): 1–23.

———. 1997. Grammatical Structures in Verb Serialization. In Alex Alsina (ed.), Complex Predicates, pp. 289–354. Stanford, Calif.: Center for the Study of Language and Information.

Egesdal, Steven M. 1981. Some Ideas on the Origin of Salish Lexical Suffixes. University of Hawaii Working Papers in Linguistics 13: 3–19.

Emanatian, Michele. 1988. The Nootka Passive Revisited. In William Shipley (ed.), In Honor of Mary Haas, pp. 265–291. Berlin: Mouton de Gruyter.

Foley, William A., and Mike Olson. 1985. Clausehood and Verb Serialization. In Johanna Nichols and Anthony C. Woodbury (eds.), Grammar Inside and Outside the Clause, pp. 17–60. Cambridge: Cambridge University Press.

Foley, William A., and Robert D. Van Valin. 1984. Functional Syntax and Universal Grammar. Cambridge: Cambridge University Press.

Givón, T. 1984. Syntax: A Functional-Typological Introduction, Vol. 1. Amsterdam: John Benjamins.

———. 1991. Serial Verbs and the Mental Reality of 'Event': Grammatical vs. Cognitive Packaging. In Elizabeth C. Traugott and Bernd Heine (eds.), Approaches to Grammaticalization, pp. 81–128. Philadelphia: John Benjamins.

Golla, Susan M. 1987. He Has a Name: History and Social Structure among the Indians of Western Vancouver Island. Ph.D. dissertation, Columbia University.

Greenberg, Joseph H. 1963. Some Universals of Grammar with Particular Reference to the Order of Meaningful Elements. In Joseph H. Greenberg (ed.), Universals of Language, pp. 73–113. Cambridge, Mass.: MIT Press.

Haas, Mary R. N.d. A List of Nootkan Cognates.

———. 1969a. Internal Reconstruction of the Nootka-Nitinat Pronominal Suffixes. International Journal of American Linguistics 35(2): 108–124.

———. 1969b. Stem Extenders in Nootka-Nitinat. Paper presented at the Fourth International Conference on Salish Languages, University of Victoria.

———. 1972. The Structure of Stems and Roots in Nootka-Nitinat. International Journal of American Linguistics 38(2): 83–92.

Halpern, Aaron L. 1992. Topics in the Placement and Morphology of Clitics. Ph.D. dissertation, Stanford University.

Hopper, Paul J. 1988. Emergent Grammar and the A Priori Grammar Principle. In Deborah Tannen (ed.), Linguistics in Context: Connecting Observation and Understanding, pp. 117–134. Norwood, N.J.: Ablex.

Hopper, Paul J., and Sandra Thompson. 1984. The Discourse Basis for Lexical Categories in Universal Grammar. Language 60: 703–752.

Hopper, Paul J., and Elizabeth C. Traugott. 1993. Grammaticalization. Cambridge: Cambridge University Press.

Jacobsen, William H., Jr. 1969a. Labialization in Nootkan. Paper presented at the Fourth International Conference on Salish Languages, University of Victoria.

———. 1969b. Origin of the Nootka Pharyngeals. International Journal of American Linguistics 35(2): 125–153.

———. 1973. The Pattern of Makah Pronouns. Paper presented at the Eighth International Conference on Salish Languages, University of Oregon.

———. 1976. Wakashan. Paper presented at the Northwest Coast Studies Conference, Simon Fraser University.

———. 1979a. Noun and Verb in Nootkan. In Barbara S. Efrat (ed.), The Victoria Conference on Northwestern Languages, pp. 83–155. British Columbia Provincial Museum Heritage Record 4. Victoria, B.C.: British Columbia Provincial Museum.

———. 1979b. Wakashan Comparative Studies. In Lyle Campbell and Marianne Mithun (eds.), The Languages of Native America: Historical and Comparative Assessment, pp. 766–802. Austin: University of Texas Press.

———. 1993. Subordination and Cosubordination in Nootka: Clause Combining in a Polysynthetic Verb-Initial Language. In Robert D. Van Valin, Jr. (ed.), Advances in Role and Reference Grammar, pp. 235–274. Amsterdam: John Benjamins.

Kinkade, M. Dale. 1983. Salish Evidence against the Universality of 'Noun' and 'Verb'. Lingua 60: 25–40.

Klaiman, M. H. 1992. Inverse Languages. Lingua 88: 227–261.

Klavans, Judith L. 1983. The Morphology of Cliticization. Paper presented at the Parasession on the Interplay of Phonology, Morphology and Syntax, Chicago Linguistic Society.

———. 1985. The Independence of Syntax and Phonology in Cliticization. Lg 61(1): 95–120.

Klokeid, Terry J. 1972. An Introduction to the West Coast Languages of Vancouver Island. Ms.

———. 1975. Abstractness and 'Variable Vowels' in Tseshaht. Paper presented at the Canadian Linguistic Association Annual Meeting, Edmonton.

———. 1976. Encliticization in Nitnaht. Paper presented at the Eleventh International Conference on Salish Languages, University of Washington.

———. 1978. Surface Structure Constraints and Nitinaht Enclitics. In Eung-Do Cook and Jonathan Kaye (eds.), Linguistic Studies of Native Canada, pp. 157–176. Vancouver, B.C.: University of British Columbia Press.

———. 1990. Variable Length and Persistently Long Vowels in Southern Wakashan. Paper presented at the 25th International Conference on Salish and Neighbouring Languages, University of British Columbia.

Klokeid, Terry J., and Kathleen A. Mooney. 1970. The Source of Prepositional Phrases in Nootka. Ms.

Kuipers, Aert. 1968. The Categories Verb-Noun and Transitive-Intransitive in English and Squamish. Lingua 21: 610–626.

Langacker, Ronald W. 1987. Foundations of Cognitive Grammar, Vol 1: Theoretical Prerequisites. Stanford, Calif.: Stanford University Press.

Levine, Robert D. 1980. On the Lexical Origin of the Kwakwala Passive. International Journal of American Linguistics 46(4): 240–258.

———. 1984. Empty Categories, Rules of Grammar, and Kwakwala Complementation. In Eung-Do Cook and Donna B. Gerdts (eds.), Syntax and Semantics 16: The Syntax of Native American Languages, pp. 215–245. New York: Academic Press.

Li, Charles N. 1976. Subject and Topic. New York: Academic Press.

Li, Charles N., and Sandra A. Thompson. 1976. Subject and Topic: A New Typology of Language. In Charles N. Li (ed.), Subject and Topic, pp. 457–490. New York: Academic Press.

Lord, Carol. 1973. Serial Verbs in Transition. Studies in African Linguistics 4(3): 269–296.

Mithun, Marianne. 1984. The Evolution of Noun Incorporation. Language 60(4): 847–894.

———. 1987. Is Basic Word Order Universal?. In Russel Tomlin (ed.), Coherence and Grounding in Discourse, pp. 217–262. Amsterdam: John Benjamins.

Nakayama, Toshihide. 1993. On the Behavior of Suffixes in Nuuchahnulth. Paper presented at the 28th International Conference on Salish and Neighbouring Languages, University of Washington.

———. 1994. Phrasal Suffixation in Nootka. In Osahito Miyaoka (ed.), Languages of the North Pacific Rim, pp. 263–272. Sapporo: Department of Linguistics, Hokkaido University.

———. 1995a. Functional Characteristics of Object in Nootka. Paper presented at the Summer Meeting of the Society for the Study of the Indigenous Languages of the Americas, University of New Mexico.

———. 1995b. Implications of Typological Characteristics for the Nature of Argument Structure: The Case of a Polysynthetic Language. Paper presented at the International Conference on Functional Approaches to Grammar, University of New Mexico.

———. 1997a. Discourse-Pragmatic Dynamism in Nootka Morphosyntax. Ph.D. dissertation, University of California, Santa Barbara.

———. 1997b. Functions of the Nootka (Nuuchahnulth) Passive Suffix. International Journal of American Linguistics 63(3): 412–431.

Nichols, Johanna, and Anthony C. Woodbury (eds.). 1985. Grammar Inside and Outside the Clause. Cambridge: Cambridge University Press.

Pawley, Andrew. 1987. Encoding Events in Kalam and English: Different Logics for Reporting Experience. In Russel Tomlin (ed.), Coherence and Grounding in Discourse, pp. 329–360. Amsterdam: John Benjamins.

———. 1993. A Language Which Defies Description by Ordinary Means. In William A. Foley (ed.), The Role of Theory in Language Description, pp. 87–129. Berlin: Mouton de Gruyter.

Payne, Doris L. 1987. Information Structuring in Papago Narrative Discourse. Language 63(4): 783–804.

Rosch, Eleanor H. 1973. On the Internal Structure of Perceptual and Semantic Categories. In T. E. Moore (ed.), Cognitive Development and the Acquisition of Language, pp. 111–144. New York: Academic Press.

Rose, Suzanne M. 1976. Lenition and Glottalization in Nootka. M.A. thesis, University of Victoria.

———. 1981. Kyuquot Grammar. Ph.D. dissertation, University of Victoria.

Rose, Suzanne M., and Barry F. Carlson. 1984. The Nootka-Nitinaht Passive. Anthropological Linguistics 26(1): 1–12.

Sapir, Edward. N.d. Unpublished field notes. Franz Boas Collection. Philadelphia: American Philosophical Society Library.

———. 1911a. Some Aspects of Nootka Language and Culture. American Anthropologist 13: 15–28.

———. 1911b. The Problem of Noun Incorporation in American Languages. American Anthropologist 13: 250–282.

———. 1915. Abnormal Types of Speech in Nootka. Canada Department of Mines, Geological Survey. National Museum of Canada Memoir 62. Ottawa: Government Printing Bureau.

———. 1916. Time Perspective in Aboriginal Culture: A Study in Method. Canada Department of Mines, Geological Survey. National Museum of Canada Memoir 70. Ottawa: Government Printing Bureau.

———. 1921. Language. New York: Harcourt Brace Jovanovich.

———. 1924. The Rival Whalers, a Nitinat Story. International Journal of American Linguistics 3(1): 76–102.

Sapir, Edward, and Morris Swadesh. 1939. Nootka Texts: Tales and Ethnological Narratives with Grammatical Notes and Lexical Materials. Philadelphia: Linguistic Society of America.

———. 1955. Native Account of Nootka Ethnography. International Journal of American Linguistics 21 (4), Part 2.

Sherzer, Joel. 1976. An Areal-Typological Study of American Indian Languages of North of Mexico. Amsterdam: North-Holland.

Swadesh, Morris. 1933. Internal Economy of the Nootka. Ph.D. dissertation, Yale University.

———. 1939. Nootka Internal Syntax. International Journal of American Linguistics 9(2–4): 77–102.

———. 1948. A Structural Trend in Nootka. Word 4(2): 106–119.

Thomas, Alexander, and Eugene Y. Arima. 1970. T'a:t'a:qsapa — A Practical Orthography for Nootka. National Museum of Man, Publication in Ethnology. Ottawa: National Museums of Canada.

Thompson, Laurence C., and M. Dale Kinkade. 1990. Languages. In Wayne Suttles (ed.), Handbook of North American Indians, Vol. 7: Northwest Coast, pp. 30–51. Washington, D.C.: Smithsonian Institution.

Touchie, Bernice N. 1977. Nitinaht. International Journal of American Linguistics, Native Texts Series 2(3): 69–97.

Van Valin, Robert D., Jr. 1993. A Synopsis of Role and Reference Grammar. In Robert D. Van Valin, Jr. (ed.), Advances in Role and Reference Grammar, pp. 1–164. Amsterdam: John Benjamins.

Walbran, John T. 1909. British Columbia Coast Names. Ottawa: Government Printing Bureau.

Whistler, Kenneth W. 1980. Inverse Person Marking in Nootkan. Ms.

———. 1985. Focus, Perspective, and Inverse Person Marking in Nootkan. In Johanna Nichols and Anthony C. Woodbury (eds.), Grammar Inside and Outside the Clause, pp. 227–265. Cambridge: Cambridge University Press.

Zwicky, Arnold M., and Geoffrey K. Pullum. 1983. Cliticization vs. Inflection: English *n't*. Language 59(3): 502–513.

www.ingramcontent.com/pod-product-compliance
Lightning Source LLC
Chambersburg PA
CBHW060242240426
43673CB00048B/1942